America...
I'm Talking to You

Wes Ifan

WJV Publishing/Bookbaby Publishing
Published in the United States of America October 2011
ISBN: 978-1-105-26515-0

America...I'm Talking to You Copyright © 2011 Iorwuese Ifan. All rights reserved

America...I'm Talking to You

Contents

FOREWORD	2
CHAPTER ONE: Opening Remarks	4
CHAPTER TWO: Who Am I?	10
CHAPTER THREE: We The People	30
CHAPTER FOUR: Politics as Usual	49
CHAPTER FIVE: It Was All a Dream	58
CHAPTER SIX: Whose Country is this?	83
CHAPTER SEVEN: The Future Starts Today	99
CHAPTER EIGHT: Closing Remarks	114
EPILOGUE:	121
NOTES:	124
ACKNOWLEDGMENTS:	129

Foreword

"We do big things. From the earliest days of our founding, America has been the story of ordinary people who dare to dream. That's how we win the future." President Barack Obama State of the Union Address 2011

During a season of economic fragility in the United States of America, the country has reached a turning point where the only true option of rebuilding America is to invest within. This country has been a leader of the free world because we dare to dream. As ordinary people we are innovative and committed to fulfilling our destiny.

Wes Ifan tackles the challenges that have plagued America in the last decade to engage in an honest dialogue of how to begin the long road toward recovery from the brink of economic despair. In his heartfelt, open letter <u>America...I'm Talking to You</u>, Ifan offers solutions that all citizens can embrace to contribute to stabilizing our great nation.

Empathy for people less fortunate, advocating for entrepreneurs, staunch support of a vibrant educational system and investing in the middle class is what made this nation superior.

While our priorities have been misplaced somewhat, this book serves as a gentle reminder of what separates us from the rest of the world.

In reading this book, I believe all individuals will walk away recognizing that we are collectively responsible for the state of our country. We have a moral obligation to preserve the right to pursue our dreams and our destiny without excuse. We are creative, we are resilient and we are the standard of excellence. If there is a fundamental flaw between where we stand and what we desire, we have an obligation to correct that flaw.

This book is a call to action-will you respond? Will you dare to dream? Will you utilize your God-given talent to pursue destiny? When we join forces collectively after an honest discussion, we make it difficult for other nations to compete. I am an ordinary individual who dares to dream and I know we will win the future!

Nicole B. Simpson, CFP

Author of Dare 2 Dream…Pushing Past Your Pain to Pursue Purpose
9/11/01 A Long Road Toward Recovery

Chapter 1
Opening Remarks

"Wake up America! I am here to say that we can't continue to be divided!" excerpt from "Opening Remarks" off my album America...I'm Talking to You

When I finally sat down to collect my thoughts and to write this manuscript, I began to ask myself the question...as a naturalized citizen of this great country, America, what could I possibly say to positively affect the lives of the individuals who will pick up and read this book? To begin, I surmised to myself that my clear purpose on this earth is to lead others to their God given potential while leaving a positive and spiritual impact on their lives. To this end, I decided it might be useful to say something, possibly, that speaks to everyone who will not only read this book, but who might, by a very slim happenstance, come in contact with me. So, whether it is the social, economic or political commentary that I make here, I intend for it to not only be truthful, but also educational and uplifting. Above all, it should reveal the glory of my Creator that is within me. It is my hope that you will see, feel and agree.

I am not a politician who has worked on extensive legislation. I haven't been elected to a local, state, or federal office; at least not at the point of writing this manuscript. I am, however, a concerned citizen who has volunteered my time and energy for the causes that I felt would contribute to the common good. I have seen some things in my adult life thus far and I've made a few observations I'd like to share with you for your consideration.

The following is further background on what I hope to accomplish through this book. My first goal is to share my upbringing here in America. While I was not born in the United States, I was raised here from the age of less than one. I have been a citizen for fifteen years. I know the American story fully well. I have enjoyed the freedoms of life, liberty, and the pursuit of happiness. My story is no different than anybody else in this great country. I feel it will be useful for people to understand my story and the unique experiences I have had. This must precede everything else that is to come because it will provide a context.

America...I'm Talking to You

My next goal is to dive into the social structure of this country; the stratification of it, and then talk about the political influences on this phenomenon. Social stratification is the separation of the society into upper, middle, and lower class. Much of our local, state, and federal government decisions directly impact the various social strata in very impressive ways. What I also find to be particularly interesting is the strength and viability of special interest groups and their impact on national politics. By special interest groups, I don't mean Mothers Against Drunk Driving. I'm talking about the big time corporations that always seem to have their hands in every important policy decision. It seems that in the politics of today, votes can be bought with the almighty dollar. The recent ruling by Supreme Court on the ability of corporations to spend limitless amounts of money to endorse candidates of their choosing, without sometimes as much as revealing their identities, as a terrible corrupting of our democratic processes. It is easy to see and to feel the political grip of these corporations around the proverbial throat of democracy. It seems inconceivable to me that we can seriously discuss a system for the people by the people under those circumstances, unless, of course, you took the viewpoint of one of the primary contestants for the presidency who said "corporations are people"; a rather simplistic and inaccurate portrayal. It would more appropriately be described as a system for the corporations on the backs of the people.

I'd also like to talk about the American Dream and the role of young people in government moving forward. I'd like to discuss an idea that I always talk about with my friends..."The Paradigm Shift". The Presidential election of 2008 was such an event. It was a generational shift from the Baby Boomers and Generation X to Generation Y. Although there are some who are afraid of this shift, the fact remains that Generation Y is rapidly becoming the most influential Generation in the Western world and they have to take leadership control and restore the American Dream in my estimation and I will discuss why.

Finally, I'll answer the question...where do we go from here? I want to give some thoughtful commentary on what I think we have to do as a country to move to the next level of leadership in the world today. One such theory is the idea of restoring our egalitarian philosophy that the founding fathers professed in the declaration of independence…"all men were created equal".

Our forefathers talked at great length about the injustice of birthright in the English monarchy. As such they continued to focus on the Enlightenment philosophy that all people had "inalienable rights endowed by the creator". It was this philosophy that became the bedrock of the U.S. Constitution and The Bill of Rights. I remain enamored by the principles of egalitarianism, most especially perhaps because it falls in line with my Christian upbringing. I am surprised to hear others who say that they share the same Christian belief but reject this philosophy of egalitarianism; however that discussion is for another time.

What you will see throughout this book is a common thread of what I like to call "principled purpose". Principled purpose allows us to have useful dialogue about issues and to debate them so as to reach a consensus about how to move forward. In the early days of this great nation, principled purpose was the method with which the original Articles of Confederation were drafted. Principled purpose allowed the founding fathers to have foresight enough to know where the responsibilities of government ended and the rights of individuals began. Principled purpose allowed this Union to continue to perfect itself into a better image. This is the same principled purpose that I will use to make the points presented in this book; not partisan thoughts or political buzzwords; merely common sense. In my estimation that is what is missing in political discourse these days...common sense! America...I'm talking to you!

Chapter 2
Who Am I?

"I am fearfully and wonderfully made!"

My name is Iorwuese Ifan. I was born on February 18, 1981 in the country of Nigeria. Most of my friends and colleagues know me as Wes. I am the son of a mother (Zanenge Ifan) and father (Agber Ifan) who have spent every waking hour of my life trying to teach me, mold me, and to provide for me. I have spent all but 10 months of my life here in the United States. In 1980, my dad was accepted into the PhD program at the University of Wisconsin (Madison). Soon after I was born, my dad would bring my mom and me across the Atlantic to the United States of America. We came to America without much and with no extended family to rely upon. The great thing about America is that such a circumstance does not have to limit you. You can make your dreams come true and anything is possible with hard work, education, and determination. These are principles that my parents tried to instill in me from a very young age.

America...I'm Talking to You

My unique American story begins with my father's journey. He came to the U.S. in 1980 with less than $2,000 in his pocket. He arrived at JFK Airport in New York City, and had to hitch a taxicab from there to LaGuardia, also in New York City, to catch a connecting flight to Milwaukee, Wisconsin, and then to the Dane County Airport in Madison, Wisconsin. Unbeknownst to him, the taxicab ride to LaGuardia would cost him $60! This was a clear case of mischief and outright theft by an unscrupulous taxicab driver. To say my father was shocked is an understatement; but the incident introduced him to some elements of so-called free market forces and the unscrupulous elements that exist within it; those who are bent on exploiting people who don't know any better. On a personal level, it taught my father that he had to be on guard, which he has since then only rarely let down.

My father to this day is not shy about going after the penny that he believes someone is cheating him out of. He asks plenty of questions when someone says that they are going to provide a service for him. He wants to know up front how the price is being calculated so that he can determine for himself if it is worth what this individual is saying it's worth. This, and other similar experiences, has shaped my father's outlook on price negotiation and bargaining. It is said that experience is life's greatest teacher, and my father had begun to learn several lessons in the first 48 hours of being here in the United States. Recall that he came to the U.S. with less than $2,000 which was supposed to last for another 6 weeks. He had to secure an apartment, get himself situated, and live off this money until a stipend arrived from Nigeria for his education and other expenses. Just imagine that!

The very first phone call that my father received from Nigeria, which came approximately a month after his arrival to America, was another defining moment of his early days in his new country. That phone call was from my paternal grandfather, who called to let my father know that I was born. However, within that same phone conversation, my father was also informed about the death of his mother – my paternal grandmother. I was born two days to the passing to glory of my grandmother! Here you have the jubilation of a new life coming into the world juxtaposed with the agonizing realization that the woman who nurtured you for most of your life is no longer here. My father at that moment would've left this country if he had a plane ticket, but he didn't have that option. The money that he was supposed to receive as a stipend for his education and other expenses was not going to get here for several more weeks. What little money he had arrived in the new country with was severely depleted by now; it was barely enough to survive on, much less to purchase a return ticket to Nigeria. These new developments made for a very dicey situation and it also underscored the value of the $60 he spent getting to LaGuardia back in New York City. My grandfather had called my father from a pay phone at the Nigerian postal, telecommunication (P&T) center. That is, there was no way to make a return call directly from America back to my grandfather. Given the shock of the bits of news from my grandfather, my father hadn't the mental composure to ask if he needed to be home for my grandmother's funeral. Not that he had the means to go even if that was required. Nevertheless, my father sent a telegram to my grandfather asking if he needed come back home. My father was seeking affirmation from my grandfather to leave America, and to go back home. If grandfather had approved, then he might have sent along a plane ticket too. Instead what my father got was sort of a rebuke from my grandfather – said my grandfather "The last time I checked, you weren't Jesus! I don't know what value you can bring by leaving school to come home because you can't raise your mother from the dead!" Essentially, my grandfather was telling my father to go on and live his life and make something of himself. Perhaps that was the best way to honor the legacy of my grandmother. It turned out that my father's academic performance for that semester was helped by this; he had the best grades of his academic pursuit that semester. My father admits that he blocked out the rest of the world and focused on his studies. As difficult as it was to deal with the pain of the loss, he was able to overcome.

By late 1981, the focus of my father when he came home to Nigeria to get me and my mother was to strengthen the family nucleus, devise a useful means of survival, and to focus on academic pursuit. My parents wanted to make sure that I was provided for since I was only an infant. To account for that, my father purchased a health insurance policy to cover my mother and me. He did that for two years because once he got a teaching assistantship position, he was able to cover us through the benefits afforded by the university. My mother and father became very proficient at survival given the meager resources that they had at the time. They budgeted well by cutting coupons and looking for sales. I remember my mother sharing a story with me about how they used to buy winter clothes when they were on clearance in the spring and summer and then buy summer clothes when they were on clearance in the fall and winter. My father said that he had to be disciplined like this because we didn't have any rich uncles or aunts to bail us out. It was just us. Again, they were focused on strengthening the family nucleus. If he didn't provide for the family, then we would be out of luck and on the street.

My mother even worked as a housekeeper at one of the hotels to supplement the income that my father was getting from his teaching assistant position. My father told me a story once of how he took us to K-Mart on the Southside of Madison and my mother was looking for a pair of shoes that she would be using for work. She went and found a pair that she wanted to try on. Not only did she try on the shoe, but she got down on her hands and knees in the aisles of the store to mimic what she would be doing if she were cleaning the floors at the hotel. She was doing this to get a sense of how the shoe felt if she were actually doing the job. To my father it almost brought tears to his eyes because my mother came from a family that was well off in Nigeria. She was not required to do the sort of manual labor that she was now doing. My father was a pharmacist in Nigeria and had a life that was considered middle class in all aspects. My grandfather was even a medical health superintendant and supervised several rural clinics in Nigeria. For my father to watch my mother demonstrate how she would be cleaning floors and toilets was a life altering realization for him. He did not want her to have to do that anymore and it raised his resolve to levels that may have surprised even him. My father quickly realized that if he didn't want my mother working as a housekeeper then he would have to complete his studies and get the best possible job, watch every penny, and budget relentlessly. All of these experiences drive his behavior as well as what he would teach his children in life. These experiences taught my father that he had to be very careful with his money and save, save, save!

As a family, we faced more hardship the year my brother was born. In August of 1985, not only was my brother born, but my aunt; my father's sister passed away. My father and she were very close and this was the kind of setback that took a toll on my father because it represented another close relationship that he could not rely on as he tried to navigate life here in the America. By 1987, it was time to move on from the state of Wisconsin. Originally, the plan was to go back to Nigeria, where my father would teach at his alma mater. It even went as far as him receiving the letter of appointment. However, the University budget had been cut severely and, as a result, my father was told that he would have to pay his way back to his employment in Nigeria and then be reimbursed whenever money was available. That wasn't his expectation from the onset. He decided at that point to look for a job and eventually took a post-doctoral position at Schering Plough Research Institute in Kenilworth, New Jersey.

As my father began to get his footing in the pharmaceutical industry, he became hesitant to make any drastic moves. He became rather methodical in how he approached his finances and his professional advancement. He wanted to be sure not to create any waves so that he could avoid layoff. Juxtaposed with the reality that career advancement had to be on hold for the time being was the growing reality that we couldn't remain at the two family duplex that we were renting in Linden, New Jersey. The landlord's son was particularly a thorn in my father's side and this became a rallying point for him to really go after the purchase of a house. It is said that God works in mysterious ways. Oh, how true that is because my parents received a blessing totally unexpectedly just at the time when the harassment from the landlord et al became unbearable. My father's employer, realizing they were grossly underpaying him, upped his salary after about seven months of my father being in their employ. But not only was the salary upped, my father was then paid the arrears of salary from the previously elapsed months. This then became the seed money that was to be used for the purchase of a new home.

My parents finally settled on purchasing a home in Piscataway, NJ. It was a nice ranch style house with a fenced in backyard, a one car garage, and a pool in the back. It was the picture of the American Dream. We had finally made it after all the toil and strain of paycheck to paycheck living (which still exists today I might add). There was no more landlord; no more landlord's son harassing us and telling us we can't play in the yard. We finally achieved the dream of home ownership. Once again, however, tragedy would strike our family and this time my maternal grandmother passed away. Since my parents had already put money down on the house, they had no funds for my mother and my little sister, who was only six months by now to go back to attend the funeral services and mourn the loss. Once again, struggle and strife would come because of finances. What could we do? We received some assistance from the First Baptist Church of Cranford/Elizabeth, where we worshipped and were able to attend the funeral service for grandmother.

My mother struggled with the loss of my grandmother. Even when she returned from Nigeria, it was something that continued to be on her mind. Many of the activities that she enjoyed most; cooking, sewing, and baking reminded my mother of grandma. The loss really hit home for several reasons. For one, she was very close to my grandmother and really adored her and looked up to her. My mother relished the opportunities to talk to her and to get her advice. It was very tough to adjust to the reality of not having her around. I could tell that a piece of my mother was gone because I could see the anguish in her eyes and it hurt me even as a child to see my mother struggling like that emotionally. The unfortunate thing was that we couldn't even catch our breath after her passing because very soon after that my father got a message about the passing of his father – my paternal grandfather. The complication now was that my parents had begun the permanent residency application process. It was unclear whether it was advisable to leave given the pending application.

My father came to the conclusion that his brothers should go ahead and lay my grandfather to rest. They did exactly that. Eventually the lawyers got back to him and said that he could go, but at this point he had no money to go even if he wanted to. Norman Jordan was a good friend of my father. He owned a bus company and seemed well to do. He took a liking to my father and once he heard that this was the situation, he did one of the most remarkable things that I can think of...he loaned my dad $2,000 and told him to go. He said my father could figure out how to pay him back when he returned. I thought this was rather generous of the man. Off my dad went to Nigeria to visit the family members and mourn the loss of grandpa. My father and mother are both very resilient human beings. My father has had to endure the pain of losing two parents while away in another country. Not only that, but he didn't even have the benefit of closure. Remember he couldn't attend his mother's funeral, nor could he attend his father's funeral. He wasn't able to truly get closure which comes from seeing the casket lowered into the ground. This is a burden that he bears even today.

As a son, I observed the resolve that my parents had in such difficult circumstances. I observed the determination to make my life and the life of my siblings better. I was able to see how their faith kept them from faltering even when the chips were down and they seemed to be out of luck. It pains me, when I hear stories about people abusing drugs and alcohol as a method to deal with the anguish in their life. I'm troubled when I hear people speak so pessimistically about their life circumstances. It's almost as if when you try to encourage them, they are looking at you as if you have no idea what it is like to struggle. It's as if, since the beginning of time, trials and tribulations never existed until it happened to them. Never mind the fact that we are who we are because of the sum of our life experiences. Some of those experiences will be good and some will be bad, but the idea is to take something from each experience and make the most of them.

I've been able to witness the constructive way to deal with tough circumstances and because of that, I've been able to deal with tough circumstances in my life differently. My demeanor and outlook on life doesn't come from some misconception that everything is alright all the time. It also isn't rooted in some fairy tale where you live happily ever after. My mother and my father have been able to provide a frame of reference to draw upon and because of the example my parents set, I understand that trouble doesn't last always. I understand that morning will come after the darkness and that the sunshine will come after the rain.

●●●●●

America...I'm Talking to You

The great thing about my life is that it isn't all hardship. I've told many people the reason that I am who I am is in large part because my parents provided structure and safety. Those are the two greatest gifts that any parent can give to their children. Structure teaches a child that everything has its place and reason. It causes a child to know that there is a time for everything much like the third chapter in the Biblical book of Ecclesiastes tells us. Safety nurtures a child's ability to be just that...a child. Nowadays children grow up too fast it seems and this can be detrimental to their development. My parents indirectly created a blueprint for how to raise children and although I was their first "experiment" they did a heck of a job.

The structure began from the time I was little. When my father would go off to class or work, my mother stayed home with me and did everything that she could to instill a sense of education and accomplishment. She read books to me constantly. At times, I wasn't even sure that I understood fully what she was reading to me. The important thing was that she was here for me; constantly nurturing and teaching me. That structure continued even when we moved to Linden and eventually when we moved to Piscataway. It wasn't that my mother didn't work because she did. Her priority though was to make sure that she was home to put us on the bus in the morning and to see us when we got home from school. This is the type of sacrifice that she made as a parent to ensure that we had structure. It is something that I feel is disappointingly absent in today's society. There are several economic factors that contribute to that trend, but let's face it America, we can do better. We can do better for ourselves and for our children. It just takes discipline and a laser like determination on the part of parents.

Safety came in the form of a stable marriage and a stable home. Marriage as an institution has suffered a great deal over the last 30 years. There are some who would suggest that it has more to do with same gender marriages, but I would contend that marriage as an institution was imploding well before this debate even came onto the scene. The reasons for which are well documented; however I will not get into that discussion here. The point is, my parents believe in marriage and have continued to abide by their vows, and that has provided safety for me and my siblings. My safety also came from the fact that my parents were always keeping an eye out for what would be the best environment to raise us in. Once Linden became a burden and his children couldn't play outside freely, my dad decided it was time to move to Piscataway. Once the neighborhood in Piscataway got a little sketchy, we were on the move to Hillsborough, NJ. It was never about what was best for my parents. They were always trying to figure out how to ensure the best for their kids. Sometimes you have to forget about yourself for a minute and ask whether or not the decisions you make are going to help your children. Structure and safety have a tremendous impact on the development of your children. I'm one of the lucky ones…I came from tremendous structure and safety and I'm better off for it.

There was something else that my parents wanted to do as well. They wanted to create the environment where we were unafraid to develop our talent. They wanted to create an environment within the household that encouraged us to aspire to great things. They wanted us to work hard, stay focused, and pay attention to details and this, more so than anything else, became my identity. I never really knew anything else. I knew that I had to be willing to work ten times harder than the average person to get what I wanted. I suppose I didn't really know the implications of such thinking at the time. I was merely trying to emulate what I was seeing before me.

I can recall an incident entering my freshman year of high school. At the end of August, incoming freshmen and their parents could come to Piscataway High School and take a tour of the school and get introduced to the teachers that they would have for the year. My father and I went and we were enjoying the tour of the school. We eventually came to my Algebra 2 class and we were immediately greeted by the teacher (here we'll just call her Anna). Anna's first question to us was "Are you in the right place? This is Algebra 2." My father was not too pleased by this line of questioning because it was as if she was questioning my legitimacy as an algebra student. My father told me at that point that it was necessary for me to work ten times harder than everyone else to achieve the highest levels of success. That was just one of many wise sayings my dad would share with me.

America...I'm Talking to You

My father had several wise sayings that he picked up as he grew up in Nigeria and he would often recite them to my siblings and me. He would always tell us that "stupidity is contagious. Don't just follow the crowd, but exercise the power of independent self thought and decision making"; or "we must be willing to work in order to get what we want". My mother would always tell me, "my son you can be anything that you want to be". She would remind me to never short change myself and accept less than what I was worth. If she felt that I wasn't getting a fair shake at school, she'd talk to the teacher. If she felt that I wasn't being paid fairly at a job, she'd tell me to find another one.

This is what makes my parents so great. They never stop teaching. They never stop giving advice. They never stop caring. It's funny that when I was a teenager, I wanted them to stop telling me what to do, but yet I wanted them to care when it was beneficial to me. As I got into my 20's, I started to understand more fully the lessons they were trying to teach me when I was younger. I now find myself asking more questions as an adult to hear their perspective. Some people never learn that lesson, and others learn it when it's too late. My father lamented to me once that he often wishes his father was still alive so that he could pick up the phone and ask him what he would do in a situation. I have had the benefit of being able to do just that. I have been able to ask myself that question and then call dad on the phone to hear his perspective. That's the thing that I am grateful for the most. I have parents who never stopped caring. I'm positive that this is the reason that I came out the way that I did.

My story isn't that much different from anyone else's. I am trying to lead a life of purpose which means that I asked God to reveal to me what he intends for me to do. The conclusion that I arrived at was that God intends for me to effectively lead others to their God given potential while leaving a positive and spiritual impact on their life. In short, everyone I come in contact with should be better off after their interaction with the God in me.

Undoubtedly, my pursuit of such a purpose will require much sacrifice. It will also entail taking the narrow road, which is traveled by few. It can be a lonely prospect, but I have the family support and structure in place to navigate such terrain. In time, I will fulfill this purpose because I believe in one who is greater than me and is capable of doing exceedingly and abundantly more than I could ever ask or imagine. I digress though...allow me to return to the message at hand. I must now speak to America!

Chapter 3
We the People

"We the people of the United States..."

Who I am shouldn't be nearly as important as who we are. Who are we? We're Americans. The writers of the Constitution wrote the following preamble:

> *We the people of the United States, in order to form a more perfect union, establish justice, insure domestic tranquility, provide for the common defense, promote the general welfare, and secure the blessings of liberty to ourselves and our posterity, do ordain and establish this Constitution for the United States of America.*

Often times, I wonder if this is still our intent. Do we really still believe what is in the constitution? Are we intent on living out the ideals that form the basic creed of this nation? There are some who will claim that they are strong supporters of the U.S. Constitution; many of which will claim to be experts or strict adherents to it. Most if not all of these individuals often forget the fact that we have 27 amendments…and counting, added to the constitution.

If the constitution is the end all be all of moral law, why do you imagine, that we have to add amendments to ensure, for example, that minorities would not be discriminated against or denied rights to vote? Why did we have to add amendments to enforce term limits for the President? Why did we have to add an amendment to protect citizens against unlawful search and seizure? The answer is simple…we are human and imperfect; this is why the founding fathers left room for us to perfect ourselves. They realized that they didn't have all the answers. Perhaps we all can benefit from coming to the realization that the Constitution doesn't have all the answers either. It's a starting point, but we may have to make some adjustments along the road to perfection.

Perhaps a further explanation is warranted here: The preamble of the Constitution was clear in its implication that we are trying to form a more perfect union. That would suggest that it is a process. We don't become a more perfect union overnight. It takes time. What is also true is that as the union continues to perfect itself, we have to be willing as a country to adapt along with it. Martin Luther King Jr. once said that "we all came in different ships but we're all in the same boat". We all got here different ways, but it is in our common interest to do the right thing by one another. I wish that more people would think that way because I believe that the forefathers were thinking this very same thing when they wrote the preamble.

I suppose that when you're united against the Queen's tyranny, it has a way of giving everyone a single minded focus. We work together as a unit knowing that we have a common enemy. Needless to speak here, in the same vein, to the galvanizing effect on our community following the attacks of September 11, 2001; America had not been so single mindedly focused on a common enemy. In churches, fellowship is often encouraged because it creates a positive dynamic between the members. It fosters an environment that keeps everyone on one accord. The congregation can unify around the idea that we are involved in a battle against a common enemy called sin. Nowadays, it seems that pundits and media personalities would rather use the

Constitution as a bone of contention and not a unifying document that displays our purpose as a nation. They'd rather create rifts and emphasize differences instead of speaking to the commonalities we share. They'd rather discourage fellowship instead of encouraging togetherness. This needs to change in America. The extension of partisan politics and campaigning into governance and policy formulation is detrimental to the survival of our union.

Another element of the preamble that is worth focusing on is the part which says "...*promote the general welfare, and secure the blessings of liberty to ourselves and our posterity...*" In other words we want to focus on the prosperity, safety, and freedom for ourselves and future generations of Americans.

I want to focus on the first part. The prosperity of ourselves and future Americans; how do we take care of that? Well there are several ways to do so. One idea is to have the Federal Government facilitate this by providing direct support and incentives to non-profits and private citizens to promote the general welfare. Another idea is to create the conditions for individuals to succeed. That means having laws that encourage education, prohibit discrimination in the workplace and in schools, and preserving individual rights. There is still the idea of encouraging innovation and free enterprise. This approach is commonly referred to as the "trickle down" effect. If we stimulate free enterprise and encourage innovation, it will create more jobs and opportunities for the general public and thus promote the general welfare.

There are some who talk about the constitution from the viewpoint of individualism and natural rights. There are some who strongly advocate self governance and self ownership. Many of these individuals talk about smaller government, social conservatism, and laissez-faire economics. Much of the Tea Party movement in U.S. politics focuses on these aspects of the constitution. Their message to the Federal Government is to rein in spending and reduce the involvement of government in free enterprise. At the core of their belief is deficit reduction to avoid heaping too much debt on future generations thereby disrupting capitalism. I suppose for them this is the part about the *general welfare and the blessings of liberty for ourselves and our posterity.*

I don't wish to discuss the validity of left wing or right wing political ideology; however, I will offer some observations about the irony of Capitalism and how it affects our ability as a nation to execute on the preamble of our Constitution.

Capitalism, according to the *Oxford English Dictionary,* is "an economic system in which the production and distribution of goods depend on investment from private capital and profit-making". Capitalism is a *social order* where profit regulates the financial life and also the social structure. What amuses me is that people are so afraid of socialism because it represents a social order where the Government controls how much money you make. Capitalism and Socialism are both social orders. The only difference is that in Socialism the Government dictates the wealth distribution. In capitalism, the Capitalists (who in many cases are the same individuals) dictate the wealth distribution. In my opinion, capitalism is a better system because entrepreneurs have an opportunity to become influential in society. A democratic political system based upon a representative government should foster an environment where anyone can become an entrepreneur. The United States has successfully created such an environment. We built this country on capitalism but it would be wrong to believe or to suggest that the countries that practice socialism are evil. Socialism is wrong, but it is not evil. On the extreme opposite of capitalism is communism. In communism the economy is planned, i.e. the government takes total care of investment, and the distribution of goods depends on principles of equality. This is a very bad system; it eliminates the opportunity for development of the entrepreneurial spirit and, to some extent, the development of self determination. The truth about all of this, however, is that none of the systems – capitalism (the most preferred option), socialism, and communism is free. There is a cost attached to each one

Before I discuss the irony of capitalism, I think it would be wise at this juncture to bring up another irony...the idea of liberalism. Liberalism is the philosophy defending a minimalist state. In other words, liberalists promote as little governmental interference as possible and freedom of the individual. When certain basic rights such as the rights to private property and physical safety for individuals are protected, the government and its laws should not interfere. The irony lies in the use of the word liberal in today's political sphere. Liberal politics is commonly associated with increased government control and socialist economic principles. Nothing could be further from the truth.

Liberalism is defined by the belief that liberty and equality are fundamentally important. Liberalism by all intents and purposes is a belief in free and fair elections, human rights, and market economy. In fact, the American Revolution was based on this principle since the English monarchy was exercising tyranny over the colonists. Who would've thought that words could morph over time! Perhaps Americans should read up on liberalism during the Age of Enlightenment in the 18th century. They could even read about how liberalism defeated communism and fascism in the two world wars. I'll bet then we'll have some interesting dialogue between Republicans and Democrats!

At any rate, when liberalist philosophy is projected into the sphere of economics, capitalism naturally evolves as an idea: free enterprise and freedom of the individual become the ideals for business and production. Capitalism in theory is a wonderful concept. Economically it creates wealth, which leads to social mobility and material success. The only issue is that when uncontrollable greed enters the equation, it creates social disparity. Any system can become corrupted once the selfish desires of people become the driving force behind it. We've seen this happen time and time again. Totalitarian regimes are driven by an ideological premise that concentration of power makes things run better. This may be true in some instances, but you run the risk of having everything go awry if this person's moral compass goes south. The result is a dictatorship that uses the hammer of power to oppress its people and suppress their viewpoints. Capitalism is intended to do all of the right things. Its structure creates avenues for people, but if those who control the majority of wealth lose their moral compass, capitalism can become a dictatorship where wealth is the hammer instead of power. Wealth can also oppress the poor and suppress their voice because campaigns are now so heavily influenced by the wealthy!

This is the part that affects my moral psychology. I just don't understand how we can provide for the common defense, promote the general welfare, and secure the blessings of liberty to ourselves and our posterity, when we are creating the conditions for the wealthiest people to have more than entire countries. It was Dr. Cornel West who said that "the top three wealthiest individuals in the world own more than the bottom 48 countries". When you are creating disparities this huge, it is no wonder that there is such anger at corporate greed on Wall Street. It's no wonder that people are upset at government bailouts for reckless business practices. Whether you defend capitalism and neo-liberalism or not it is a fact that these disparities are a direct result of decades of capitalism in the world. More specifically, the greed of the most prominent capitalists has created these disparities. In the words of a famous (or infamous) half-first-term former Alaskan governor, I'd ask, how is that free market stuff working for ya?

I'll tell you how it's working in general. It has created the largest gap in economic wealth since the great depression. As I mentioned earlier, social stratification is the separation of the society into upper, middle, and lower class. The gap between the upper class and middle class has gotten larger; especially in the last eight to ten years. The average income of the top 5% of families is now 12 times the average income of the bottom 20%. I just don't know how that is a sustainable business model in any arena. Besides, if capitalism is dependent on profit making, wouldn't it be prudent to ensure that the consumer, responsible for purchasing your product and thus creating your profit, is financially able to support it? Wouldn't it make sense to create enough wealth in the center and bottom of the social stratum to ensure that those who own the companies can continue to make money and reinvest in their company as well as other companies?

    This is the irony of our current brand of capitalism. Capitalism generally is dependent on a steady diet of cash, to support its construct, but yet lately all it manages to do is concentrate cash at the top of the pyramid; with those who don't spend money. The super wealthy don't shop at Wal-Mart. The super wealthy don't buy groceries at the local market. The super wealthy don't support the local mom and pop businesses that you do business with each and every day in your communities. Oh, by the way, these are the businesses which are the economic engine of America. These are the businesses that employ nearly 45% of Americans. The super wealthy simply pass on their fortunes to future generations. They hoard their wealth because it gives them power. Capitalism has its merits, but it also has its vices. For one thing, it creates an atmosphere of elitism which runs counter to the egalitarian philosophy that this country was founded on. To be quite frank, elitism is the core tenet of fascism and racism. When the Nazis were trying to exterminate the Jews, it was because they had this false belief that they were better than them. Likewise, when America was at the height of Jim Crow, there was a fundamental, but false belief that Whites were better than Blacks. Elitism can create a very polarizing environment where extremist views can take root.

Another issue that arises when greed is the driving force behind capitalism is a lack of altruistic behavior. People become so focused on themselves that they cannot honor one of the basic tenets of all faiths; taking care of your neighbor. Capitalism is a system predicated on competition and as such there are winners and losers. Everyone is on their own and the reality is those with more wealth, power, and influence have more options. There is a Darwinist mentality...survival of the fittest. When you create competition, it's about me doing what I have to do to get what I need and forget about everyone else. This feeds back to the elitism that we just described. For a moment, just think about the thought process of the largest corporations. If I need to make more money, there are a couple ways that I can do it. The first is to innovate. I create a product that nobody else knows how to make and that everybody wants. I sell it and make money. That's the "hard work" approach. That was the original intent and allure of capitalism; the thought that anybody can make it if they try. The second way to make more money is to minimize cost of labor and production to make my income sheet look better to inflate profits and thus increase my stock price. Which one do you think corporations tend to lean toward? Let's just say if Enron and Qualcomm are any indications of which route corporations tend to take you decide for yourself.

At this juncture I'd like to talk about the big elephant in the room (no pun intended). There are some (mostly republicans) who talk about tax cuts as a cure all for everything that ails a sputtering economy. They feed everyone this pie in the sky mentality that if only we can keep taxes low and cut government spending that somehow all of our problems will be solved and we will create millions upon millions of jobs. Never mind the fact that tax cuts are an expense to the federal government so it's really bait and switch. It is funny how the individuals who wave the banner of fiscal responsibility always propose the most fiscally irresponsible things. At any rate, this tax cut argument is the most absurd thing I've ever heard. If that were the case, then the years between 2002 and 2008 should've been the most prosperous and innovative of all time. The single largest tax cut in American history happened within this timeframe. Did the economy grow? Did we add millions of jobs to the economy? Did we even see high single digit GDP growth? The answer to these questions is NO! The stock market went up, but it wasn't authentic. Think about it. Between 2002 and 2008, IT outsourcing alone went up 80%. Manufacturing in overseas plants increased 44%. Those jobs left the country during the time when tax cuts were meant to encourage job growth. The idea is not the thing that was wrong; once again it is greed in the mind of the capitalist that was wrong. In theory, if I am a millionaire and I own a large business that employs 400 people, a tax cut that puts more money in my pocket should mean more jobs or investment in my business that will spur job growth in other areas. If I am greedy, I pocket the money, ship jobs overseas through outsourcing and inflate my stock price in the process; thus making even more money. I can even take things a step further and keep money in off-shore accounts to evade taxes then give money to politicians who will perpetuate this cycle of greed on my behalf. In the meantime millions are left jobless and looking for jobs that may never return to the U.S.

I've also heard a lot about small businesses from the chamber of commerce and from journalists. The chatter that I hear most is that tax cuts actually help small businesses the most. This is actually true. Small businesses employ approximately 45% of America's workforce and unlike the larger multinational corporations; small businesses cannot take advantage of foreign tax credits. Small businesses are not the ones outsourcing jobs and conducting their manufacturing in underdeveloped countries. They would most certainly benefit from an extension of the Bush era tax cuts. The problem that we have is the capitalist machine that has spun out of control. How is it that larger corporations are able to have an effective tax rate that is lower than the small businesses that employ Americans right here at home? Instead of talking about tax cuts every time there is an election, we should be discussing ways to reform the tax code so that it is fairer to the businesses who keep jobs in America.

What I'd like for us to do is take a step back and ask ourselves a couple questions. One, where is the moral compass of our politics pointing? Two, who is in control of the social order we call capitalism? Clearly, overwhelming greed has gripped capitalism and has caused the disproportionate treatment that the wealthy and multinational corporations receive. Our politicians are being controlled by this aristocracy and the elected legislators further perpetuate this environment. This disproportionate treatment is rooted in significant tax favorability and huge wealth and income disparities; which are growing with each passing year. I believe it was Leona Helmsley, the queen of mean herself, who said "wealthy people don't pay taxes". The sad reality of her statement is that it is true. Those who benefit most from the tax code are the same ones benefitting from all of us screaming back and forth at one another about why we should keep tax cuts in place! America (middle and lower class) I'm talking to you! Please understand that this tax code that we argue so furiously about benefits only the top 1%.

It turns my stomach to hear some of the comments levied by many of our "beloved" radio and T.V. personalities. Many of them expressed the fact that they want the president to fail. Meanwhile I wonder to myself if people even realize that these are the people who benefit most from our passionate discord. We line their pockets as the viewership and listeners increase. We line their pockets as ad revenue flows in. They want us so consumed with fighting each other that we fail to realize that we are not following the tenets of the U.S. constitution. Times of crisis call for togetherness and single minded focus. This is the type of focus that our forefathers had when they were battling against the Queen. We need to go back to E. Pluribus Unum.

We need to do what is in the best interest of the country and its posterity. It's time to promote the general welfare and not the welfare of the few. It is time to repair the rifts that exist today.

Greed needs to be rooted out of capitalism; or at least tempered somewhat so that we can reflect the true ideals of this great country. It is clear from the trends of the last 30 years that capitalism has taken a wrong turn and contributed to a huge rift between the haves and haves not. It has created deeply entrenched hatred between different classes of people. It has hijacked our political system to the point that meaningful discussion cannot happen about how to move this country forward. Special interests have transitioned from advocacy groups for various social change agencies to huge corporate quasi-nations. We've gone from the Sierra Club to Citigroup; Green Peace to Halliburton; The Southern Poverty Law Center to Aetna. More and more, the companies with the most money are able to exercise the most influence. This is most certainly the main objective of those who have hijacked the capitalist system. Those with the most money are better than you, and their money speaks loudest!

Please do not mistake my ruminations as a call to repeal our capitalist structure. As I said before, I love capitalism because it allows us to create wealth. It is the reason my parents were able to come to the United States with nothing and eventually be able to buy their dream home and put their children through college. Capitalism is the engine that took us through the roaring 20's and economic expansion of the 1990's. My intent was to present the irony of capitalism as it relates to our constitution. I wanted to share the peril that is associated with an obsessive drive to accumulate wealth without an equally obsessive drive to create social equality. History tells us that when we neglect the social responsibility that we have to the middle class, the results are catastrophic to our economy. Not only that, but it cripples our ability to weather the type of economic storm that begun in 2008 and continued through 2009. America…I'm still talking to you!

Chapter 4
Politics as Usual

"America will never be destroyed from the outside. If we falter and lose our freedoms it will be because we destroyed ourselves"
~Abraham Lincoln

Abraham Lincoln was very profound in his insights. He is by far one of the most revered Presidents of all time. Many historians point to his cool and calm demeanor during one of the most fractured periods of this country's history. He presided over the Civil War during a time when deeply entrenched beliefs about slavery were being debated and ultimately fought over. Many would agree that what he did and how he led this country took much courage and resolve. It isn't just the fact that he freed the slaves. He took a very polarized country and brought it back together. He recognized that in order for this union to remain strong, there had to be a mending of fences. He understood the E. Pluribus Unum concept, which states that out of many we are one.

There are many historians who remain fascinated by his team of rivals concept. In fact, current U.S. President, Mr. Barack Obama mentioned this as a strong influential factor in how he chose his cabinet. There's a method to the madness because you want to be able to get the best ideas out on the table. The belief is that if you get different ideas out on the table and begin to hash them out, you'll arrive at a stronger set of solutions in the end. Political discourse in this country used to be that way.

Political discourse used to involve differing ideas and opinions being melded together to create significant legislative progress. We used to look at the process of democracy as a platform to display our strength as a nation; our ability to take a nation of immigrants and turn it into a country of the people and by the people. Now other countries sit back and watch the political bickering that has bogged down a once progressive nation. We used to be the innovators in the world; the country with bold and new ideas. Now we have regressed into a country that can't seem to get out of its own way on simple issues like how to successfully get water into a major American city within 5 days! Meanwhile other countries are able to move swiftly into action to enact legislation to respond to complex global recessionary pressures at a moment's notice. We used to be that nimble. We used to be that quick. Now all that innovation which was at the heart of our nationalism has begun to erode.

What happened to that America? Where did we go wrong? Where has our drive to be the example that other countries look to emulate gone? I've asked these questions over and over again and I came to the conclusion that we have become so transfixed with the idea of politics that we have forgotten what the purpose of politics is in the first place. The purpose of politics according to 17th century English philosopher Thomas Hobbes is "to help man escape his barbaric natural state and enjoy the benefit of civilized society". Immanuel Kant takes it a step further by stating that "a republican civil constitution must be based upon three fundamental principles: freedom, equality, and independence. Politics serves the purpose of ensuring the eventual achievement of man's natural end in a civilized society in which the people enjoy the highest possible level of freedom." Politics instead has become about one-upmanship and backstabbing.

There is an exceptional level of what I would deem immaturity among politicians on both sides of the political sphere (many of the political pundits deserve mention here as well). Kant has another piece that he wrote about enlightenment. He defines enlightenment as "man's emergence from his self-incurred immaturity." Political institutions must, as he put it, afford citizens the highest amount of freedom and the greatest level of opportunity. If these rights are guaranteed, we as a society can progress steadily toward an enlightened and progressive society; in short a better existence for all humanity. If only we could get our leaders to emerge from their state of political adolescence and stop fighting long enough to represent the will of the people; maybe we could see progress in the 21st century!

I'm not so sure that politicians are even interested in entertaining the prospect of representing the interests of the people who elected them. On second thought perhaps I'm not being fair. Politicians are representing the interests of some individuals, but I think you and I aren't *special* enough to be represented. I spoke of special interests in the previous chapter. One of the most influential special interest groups is the oil and gas industry. In 2008 they spent more than $130 Million to lobby our leadership in Washington, DC. For the eight years President George W Bush was in office, the oil industry sat back as Bush rolled back Clinton-era restrictions on the commercial uses of federal lands. They were given free access to natural preserves, national forests, and national monuments. They were almost successful in opening up drilling prospects in ANWR. Current President, Barack Obama, seemed open to expansion of off-shore drilling. The BP oil spill in the Gulf coast may have tempered his position although it has not eliminated it completely.

    I say all this to state facts…special interests such as the oil & gas industry have very cozy relationships with our politicians. I'm sure that this is something that many of us already know to be true. What is my point exactly? The point is that we as a country continue to allow greed and power to cloud our better judgment. It's the same issue we saw with the financial collapse. It's the same issue that we saw with the automobile industry in America. Campaign promises have read like a list of New Year's resolutions. They sound good, but in theory do we really expect any of them to come to fruition. I personally cannot give $3 Million to a presidential candidate but my opinions should matter. In order for politics to serve its intended purpose, the agents for that enterprise (politicians) must act toward the goal of achieving freedom for every citizen. EVERY citizen must be allowed to enjoy the highest level of freedom and not be held captive by the wants and whims of conglomerates and corporate bodies. That means that my desire for education reform shouldn't be trumped by the oil and gas industry's desire to have more access to untapped drilling reservoirs.

If you'll bear with me, I'd like to shift gears for a moment. I have gone through a detailed account of America's social construct as well as the irony of capitalism. We now find ourselves in a discussion about special interests and I wonder why special interests have such a stranglehold on the political process. Could it be that there is a reason that we seem to have this strong affinity for this type of behavior? If we took the time to think about this, you may be able to figure out where this came from. This phenomenon began in the late 1800's into the early 1900's. Max Weber published a book called the Protestant Ethic and the Spirit of Capitalism in 1905. The Weber thesis states that capitalism in northern Europe evolved when the Protestant (mainly Calvinist) ethic influenced large numbers of people to engage in work in the secular world, developing their own enterprises and engaging in trade and the accumulation of wealth for investment.

In other words, the idea of good works has been interpreted as a call to work toward successful enterprise for the purpose of accumulating wealth. This is a situation where the word of God has been perverted. It's funny how we take the words found in the Bible and try to superimpose our world view to alter the meaning. I suppose that the Protestant Ethic did not take into consideration the warning in the book of James chapter 5! In all seriousness, it's amazing how the perception of wealth is skewed. For example, there are pastors who tout prosperity ministry. They often quote John 10:10, where Jesus Christ states that he came so that we would have life and have life more abundantly. This is often mischaracterized as having more money. God wants us to live a more prosperous life, but that doesn't always mean money. It is a very dangerous proposition when you limit God to what he can do for you monetarily.

This is the culture in America though. The hunger for money is the backbone of our capitalistic society. Let's face it, America as a country has approximately 6% of the world's population, yet it owns 50% of the world's wealth. Let's break it down even further. The top 20% of the country own 85% of the country's wealth, and 42.5% of the world's wealth. This means that 42.5% of the world's wealth is being controlled by 61,401,310 people; approximately 1% of the world population!

The question you may ask is why does this matter? Why am I talking about greed, capitalism, and wealth disparities? What does this have to do with the concept of politics as usual? The answer is simple. Politicians used to answer to the people, but now they answer solely to the dollar. Whoever has the dollars has the ear of the politician and thus is able to maintain a strong grip on the political process. It is the very thing that keeps the average Joe out of the political equation. Do you realize that in 2009 special interests spent $3 Billion to lobby for governmental reforms which would benefit them?

That's more than the GDP of Liberia, Sierra Leone, and Samoa combined! Lobbyists spent more money than 3 entire countries were able to produce through their economy. It is wrong and ridiculous!

If we ever hope to restore the American Dream we are definitely going to have to change the way we do business in Washington! I'm not saying that as a political campaign slogan. I'm saying that with all seriousness. The way forward has to change and it's not going to come from the current crop of politicians. Somehow new, younger people are going to have to get involved in politics to influence *change*. Change was a big theme in the 2008 election. The only problem is that we changed the White House while Congress maintained the usual suspects. America has a new face for the franchise so to speak, but the role players are the same cast who just don't get it! I hope that somehow we can restore the American dream. I think I know how. America...I'm still talking to you!

Chapter 5
It Was All a Dream

"I look into the eyes of America, to share what is going on in all urban areas...people losing homes and I don't understand; this is not the American Dream for any man"
~excerpt from "American Dream" off of my Album America...I'm Talking to You

The American Dream was coined by James Truslow Adams in his 1931 book *Epic of America*. The point he was trying to make was that every citizen believed in their heart of hearts that they could achieve a better, richer, and happier life. It is the promise of prosperity and success that rings true in the statement that we are all created equal. It is the promise of prosperity and success that rings true in the statement that we have inalienable rights endowed by the creator which include life, liberty, and the pursuit of happiness.

At times, we've tried to attach certain status symbols to the American Dream such as home ownership. There is a danger to that because home ownership may not necessarily be the thing that will give someone life, liberty, and happiness. Instead I would contend that the American Dream ought to be whatever someone expects it to be for them. It may differ depending on who you ask. That's why we said that <u>every</u> person had the inalienable rights endowed by the creator. Each person can pursue that happiness in whatever legal way, shape, or form that they choose.

When James Truslow Adams discussed the American Dream, he was quite specific in what he meant. He stated that "the American Dream is that dream of a land in which life should be better, richer, and fuller for every man, with opportunity for each according to ability or achievement". There is a caveat to that though. He believed that it was possible for anyone to attain the fullest stature of which they are innately capable regardless of the circumstances surrounding their birth or position in life. In other words, if someone grows up poor, but they are an exceptionally gifted musician, they will be able to become wealthy. They will be able to change their life circumstances merely because they are innately capable of doing so, given their talent.

We have run into a bit of a quandary though. The American Dream isn't fully functional anymore.

America...I'm Talking to You

There are some critics who would suggest that the concept of the American Dream has set unrealistic expectations in the minds of our citizens. The fact is, the same names that you associate with "old money"; the Rockefellers, the DuPonts, the Vanderbilts, the Guggenheims, and the Rothschilds have been passing wealth on through the generations for over 125 years! The single greatest transfer of wealth is not the "redistribution of wealth" that will occur if tax rates are allowed to go back to Clinton era levels. The single greatest transfer of wealth will occur when the "old money" families transfer the inheritance to the baby boomers over the next 5 – 10 years! Four of the richest families in this country have taken a combined fortune of $ 2 – 4 Billion in 1937 and have turned it into $30 Billion by 1997 without participating heavily in the stock market! Heaven knows what that pot is worth in 2010!

What does that mean for the so called American Dream? It means that America has evolved into the very thing that they fought for so many years not to become...England! We now have an aristocracy in America. We have a social class order that looks something like this; the capitalists, the middle class, the working class, and the poor. America has become a place where social mobility is severely hampered and inheritance has become the culture. Economic opportunity is borne of inheritance and wealth transfer and not personal achievement. Moreover, innate talent is no longer a guarantee for success, because opportunity must be available to allow that talent to be nurtured. If you don't have the connections or access (which many of the wealthy families I just mentioned have) then your talent cannot be developed efficiently enough to ascend to the top. To those who believe that expiring tax cuts is somehow an attack on the American Dream, I say wake up! The fact is tax cuts, which primarily benefit the wealthiest Americans, is the second biggest transfer of wealth. Wealth was taken over time from the bottom and middle and given to the top. What that has created is one of the largest income gaps in the developed world; higher than England, Germany, and France.

Let's take an even closer look at that idea. Abraham Lincoln, in a letter to William Elkins had this to say as the Civil War was drawing to an end:

> "We may congratulate ourselves that this cruel war is nearing its end. It has cost a vast amount of treasure

and blood. . . . It has indeed been a trying hour for the Republic; but I see in the near future a crisis approaching that unnerves me and causes me to tremble for the safety of my country. As a result of the war, corporations have been enthroned and an era of corruption in high places will follow, and the money power of the country will endeavor to prolong its reign by working upon the prejudices of the people until all wealth is aggregated in a few hands and the Republic is destroyed. I feel at this moment more anxiety for the safety of my country than ever before, even in the midst of war. God grant that my suspicions may prove groundless."

Abraham Lincoln was assassinated nearly 5 months later. Look around and tell me what you see. The primary complaints that I hear from individuals claiming to be libertarian or constitutionalists are the ever increasing size of government. Meanwhile corporate entities behind the scenes undermine the very dream that you claim the government is taking from you. Again, I'm not saying that it is wrong to endeavor to make more money, but at what cost does the thirst for power, using the instrument of money, undermine the hopes and dreams of others?

When you expect that tax cuts to the wealthy are going to somehow trickle down to the rest of us, you've bought into the social construct that they would wish for you to believe. Your indifference has caused you to dream less and what we have is a situation where personal achievement is not recognized at all. You have become dependent on the upper class to pass down wealth in the form of wages for labor. As we discussed in chapter three, that is not going to happen anyway. The mere fact that we believe it will perpetuate the master-slave morality.

I'm not one for conspiracies, but I am one for commonalities. The master-slave morality as described by Friedrich Nietzsche discusses the idea that the master creates a valuable narrative; in this case the idea that tax cuts are great for everybody. They then use fear, such as the impending doom of the economy and higher jobless rates to convince you of that valuable narrative. Since the master is a person of nobility, they become the creators of the morality in which we exist. The slave morality on the other hand is a re-validation of the master's morality. We chastise those who demonize the master, and at the same time we reinforce the master's morality because it represents "the common good" so to speak. In the end, we support a theory for which there is no fundamental basis for argument. It's the same reason that blacks remained slaves in the South in the early 1800's (and remain indifferent in the face of institutional racism now). They end up believing that it's OK because the alternative is being lynched or shot (publicly chastised or denigrated). At least I have a roof over my head and the master gets his crop harvested so everybody is happy (at least there is a black President). For that slave, there is no American Dream, and for the non-wealthy the same thing is going to happen if we don't wake up!

Restoring the American Dream will take work. It will also take the fresh ideas of a new generation of politicians…a younger generation of politicians who are more pragmatic than ideological. The funny thing is that every politician on television talks about this but none of them actually *wants* to necessarily do anything about it. To hear them tell it, President Obama has been the chief opponent attacking the American Dream. Heaven forbid we actually regulate corporations, provide health care to all Americans, and invest in education and infrastructure. This notion that he has been the chief opponent of the American Dream is just false! The attack on the American Dream is the fact that social mobility is next to impossible. The attack on the

American Dream is the fact that certain school districts don't have the resources to help their students compete with students in other countries! The attack on the American Dream is the fact that corporate chief executive officers seem to believe that they should be the only source of ideas on how to improve America! They think we ordinary citizens don't know anything! Corporate executives believe that we will mess up this good thing they've got going! The American Dream is based on the idea that anyone can make it, if you only try. The social order which is dominated by capitalists makes that prospect more difficult in this country. It has nothing to do with policies, or deficits!

The question that has to be answered is how do we restore the American Dream? It seems to me that this is a difficult prospect. Thus far, we have demonstrated that the only thing that interests us at this time is creating friction between religious and ethnic groups. We infuse political rhetoric into issues that have strong influence on this country's future without providing tangible solutions to solve them. Moreover we spend countless resources, both monetary and human, on open ended military conflicts in the name of democracy. While we pour resources into these conflicts, it leaves very little money to be invested right here at home. It is frustrating that very few people are sophisticated enough to see this; or if they are, they don't care to focus on it because it is not politically expedient.

This world has become a global community and most importantly a global economy. Many of the emerging economies, especially India and China, have made tremendous strides toward becoming superpowers because they relentlessly invest in themselves; and by the way, we invest relentlessly in them too. We outsource more jobs to India and China than any other developed nation. We are also borrowing enough money from China to allow them to make interest income in the hundreds of millions! Why is America so far off course? Why are we allowing the "BRIC" economies to continue to gain ground on us competitively?

The reality is that the mid-90's was a transition period. As I always tell my brother, it was a paradigm shift. Some people may not have recognized it at the time, but we transitioned in the mid-90's from an balanced economy into a knowledge economy. Allow me to give a brief historical perspective: In the late 1700's and early 1800's, the world saw an event called the Industrial Revolution. During this time, technological and economic progress gained momentum with the development of steam-powered ships and railways. In the 1900's we saw the emergence of the internal combustion engine and the electrical power generation began. What was unique about each of these innovative periods is that the United States of America was leading the way in transformative innovation. The American economy benefited tremendously. GDP per capita continued to increase as America became the preeminent force in manufacturing. The industrial revolution brought about the emergence of the American Automotive Industry. Over time, manufacturing has left the United States because other countries began to innovate their processes and became more efficient than us at it. It was obvious that the wealth that the United States acquired during the earlier years of industrial revolution allowed us to become importers rather than exporters of goods over time.

That brings me to the mid-90's. The information age brought about a more service driven economy. You began to see dot-com companies explode onto the scene. Service industries like insurance and banking began to flourish as regulations eased. Once again the United States was a leader in this regard, but once again toward the end of the 1990's we saw that other countries again began to innovate. They became more efficient at delivering these services. Once again, American companies began to outsource these services to other countries. The only problem is that in the 21st century, we haven't begun the process of embarking on the economic frontiers of the future. Anytime this nation has been in a state of flux or transition, we have always found the resolve and ingenuity to lead the world on the path to the economic promise of the future. Unfortunately that isn't happening right now because of political wrangling and that is the source of our current stagnation.

This stagnation has incredible consequences on our economy. For one thing, it reduces the tax revenue collection for the federal government since unemployment creeps up during times of stagnation. There also tends to be an increase in government spending to keep the economy afloat until recovery can be achieved. In the meantime there is constant debate about the role of government between republicans and democrats. Republicans will contend that in tough times the role of government is to get out of the way and allow the private sector to correct itself. Democrats will contend that the role of government is to intervene to facilitate recovery in the midst of a downturn because those with the most to lose can't afford the government not to be involved. In the middle of all this argument is an inability or unwillingness to address the source of the problem in the first place. Corporate innovation is lackluster at best and business incentives haven't been reformed since the mid 70's! We have kept operating in the same mode for over 40 years expecting different results. I believe that's the definition of insanity!

Let me explain little further. The knowledge revolution began in much the same way that the industrial revolution began. We began to harness technology to produce efficiencies in business processes. Automation became even more sophisticated and information sharing became easier. The flow of knowledge was more transparent as a result and we found ourselves evolving into a knowledge based economy. The reality is that human capital became the engine of development. Unfortunately, this change doesn't favor a concentration of wealth and resources at the top. You don't have to take my word for it. There are other countries who are finding a lot of success with mixed economies who otherwise would have never been able to come close to competing with the United States. This fact alone should prompt us to figure out how to modify our approach slightly. Markets now require a more egalitarian distribution of wealth for efficient functioning.

Wealth and resource concentration at the top was a better model in the industrial revolution because it was predicated on acquisition of resources and laborers to carry out the supply chain process. That always required a significant amount of capital or access to credit capital through banks. Those who had or could acquire the most fossil fuels and industrial resources were able to control the flow of product innovation. As a result you opened up new markets, grew, and hired more people. This model is how America distanced themselves from other countries and kept us from ever being challenged much economically. We had the most wealth and thus had the ability to control the most resources. On the other hand knowledge doesn't require money; at least not in its purest sense. One would need access to adequate education, which I'll get into later, but I own the knowledge that I have in my mind.

The shift to a knowledge economy began with the transition to the information age. For better or for worse, the internet has revolutionized business. Everybody has access to the same information and therefore there aren't any distinct advantages. The only advantage is how you process that information and the efficiency with which you can provide services and "know-how" to clients. If we were to be very honest, America's past dominance was based on the fact that we had the technology or information first; thus it gave us a first-mover advantage. Our manufacturing processes were superior and thus everything was made here. All of that has changed. It is cheaper to manufacture things overseas and quite frankly other nations have prepared their workforce better to deliver knowledge based services and "know-how" because they never lost sight of the importance of education to the preparation of their workforces.

We on the other hand have continuously taken funding away from education and refuse to invest in it for the betterment of our future workforce.

Remember, the knowledge society that we have now is global in nature. It has become very innovative and is quite dependent on the use of human knowledge. You are also seeing the impact this trend is having on the use of environmental resources. The global community is becoming more conservative in their use of environmental resources; hence the "green economy" that everyone keeps referring to. When countries like China are weighing in on the use of resources and the need for conservation, you know that we are in a new age! I've noticed a more subtle change that one might not see at the surface. The political argument about capitalism and private ownership versus socialism and government ownership has become a very non-essential argument. Honestly, America still has the greatest economy and economic model. One thing that we are not good at is admitting fault and making adjustments. Because of "American Exceptionalism" we have refused to be a country that looks at ways to improve. Instead we act as if everything we do is incredible and not in need of re-tooling. That is the wrong approach especially when everything around us is changing. It's like a basketball team who is down by 10 points at halftime not making adjustments when they come back for the second half.

The reality of this discussion is that capital was scarce because it wasn't available to everyone. Those who were wealthy or had access to bank capital (that is, loans) were able to control resources. This is why capitalism was the juggernaut of economic success for so many years. Today knowledge and ideas are the "scarce" resources, but in fact they are not scarce. They are available to all who have taken it upon themselves to get a solid education. The unfortunate reality is that high school graduation rates have been stalled and in many cases decreasing. Those who try to go on to college find that costs continue to go up so fast and it is making it increasingly difficult for the average citizen to gain access. Let's not even talk about the ever increasing costs of graduate studies.

At the federal and state levels, we are reducing funding for government loans and grants further perpetuating the problem. There are some who say that teachers are the problem and standardized testing needs to be tougher when in fact, that is not the issue at all. These are just smoke and mirrors. The reality is that we are creating a society where the one resource that is available to everyone through the public education system is slowly deteriorating. If we continue to strip away public education or even worse privatize it, we are creating a situation where a resource that shouldn't be scarce at all becomes…*scarce* to its citizens! In order to compete in the 21st Century, we need to focus our attention on this source of capital…knowledge. This is the only way that we will regain and maintain our preeminence as a world super power. 20th Century traditionalists have to realize that the old argument between capitalism and socialism has changed because of education, which is the great equalizer.

    This explains why countries with socialist structures of government have been successful in participating in the latest round of economic growth. At the heart of it, knowledge based economies are not dependent on physical resources but information. To take it a step further, many countries around the world have increased their investment in knowledge specifically around education for over 20 years while we have reduced it significantly. Also by virtue of the structure of the socialist economy the distribution of wealth actually aids the efficiency of the knowledge based economy. This does not mean that America's capitalist structure is ill-equipped for the knowledge revolution. It just means that we have to be willing to make adjustments to account for the shift in the global economy much like China and India. Both countries have elements of capitalism in them, so even they recognize that it was necessary to make adjustments to their model to remain competitive on a global scale. We have a unique opportunity to beat other countries to the punch. We don't have to incorporate elements of socialism into our model, but we must make investments in the education of our workforce because education is the great equalizer of the knowledge economy.

I would say that in order to restore the American dream, we need to make minor adjustments to our economic model. We also need to revive the American manufacturing sector. It will not be easy because quality would have to improve; not to mention you'd have to lower the expectations of the unions in terms of wages and benefits. We have to reform the tax code and eliminate the loopholes that continue to reward companies who ship jobs overseas. We need to comprehensively reform the cost structure in this country and decrease some of the redundancies in regulation. Finally, we would need to have a foreign policy agenda that focuses on currency regulation. There is far too much manipulation of the American dollar currency value; especially by China. Given that we are now a global economy, something needs to be done about that because it affects trade in remarkable ways. A process like this would take several years to complete so it cannot be our only focus.

The reality is that the knowledge based economy will not go away. We as a nation must zero in on the methods that will educate our workforce; making them better equipped to compete in a global environment that is ripe with knowledge resources. Since knowledge is a tool, we have to be better, faster, and smarter at using it. We should create a new coalition of labor, business, and government leaders who will make this the chief objective of the 21st century. It remains to be seen if we have the type of leadership at all levels that will be committed to this effort. This is why I would suggest that Generation Y become much more active and involved in their civic duty to this country. Generation Y must emerge from the doldrums of apathy and walk into the necessity of activity. They need to be the ones to create the economic advantage through human capital. The driving forces of this present reality are the globalization of markets and products, as well as the complexities of information technology; both of which Generation Y is equipped to handle.

Economics no longer focuses on scarcity of capital and resources. It now focuses on scarcity of knowledge. Information can be shared without losing it and it grows through application. That also means it is important to have mechanisms in place to protect intellectual property to prevent leaks. Whether it is here, in China, or in Australia, we have to be willing to invest in the protection of our intellectual property. It amazes me that we have not put more emphasis on safeguarding our internet against hackers and those who would want to steal the identity of American citizens. I continue to be surprised that there are computer scientists and programmers in other countries who continue to outpace us in readiness against cyber-attack. 60 Minutes did an exposé on cyber terrorism in the 21st century. They pointed out that there were millions of cyber attacks that happened around the country each day. President Obama talked about revamping our high speed internet functionality and making it available to more people. These improvements will help prepare us to be competitive in a global landscape. I still question whether or not it will put us in the driver's seat as it pertains to the information economy, but at least it's a start.

Core competencies are now a key component of value in knowledge based economies. What we have to realize in this country is that the biggest threat to the United States in the 21st century is not physical threats due to terrorist attacks. The biggest threat is economic suppression; or even worse economic irrelevance. Moreover, if you look at our lack of job creation in this country there is a direct correlation between the education advancements of other countries and our decline in competitiveness on the global job front. Couple that with the increase in knowledge sharing through the internet and you have a recipe for job stagnation. In what is now a global economy, it is not enough to wrangle over the merits of supply-side versus Keynesian economics. Policy management involves a lot more than supply and demand. The externalities now have a stronger effect on macroeconomics than they did 20 years ago. In our current recession, it's not that the government hasn't done enough to help create jobs; we just aren't competitive enough in a global job market. You're not competing with fellow American citizens. You're competing with Europeans, Japanese, Indian, and Chinese professionals who are eager for a taste of the Western life. They are educating themselves and becoming more knowledgeable and we are getting our tails kicked when it comes time to interview for positions with global companies. Moreover we haven't been diligent enough at finding new industries to invest in to spur on private investment.

Since I brought up private investment, let me also discuss government spending as a matter of economic policy. Ordinarily you'll hear some politicians argue that government spending has a negative effect on the economy because it causes prices to go up and thus inflation goes up. Economic models will show this to be true and I agree with this statement. If inflation goes up then private investment goes down. This is also true, but the problem with that black and white explanation is that you aren't factoring in currency value manipulation. You haven't even taken into account trade policy agreements. You haven't taken into account that private investment may be down in the U.S. but it certainly isn't down completely because there are emerging economies elsewhere that are receiving that private investment. The old saying is that "money talks" so money goes where money can be made. In other words if the U.S doesn't invest in new lucrative industries right here in the USA, then private investment will go to the countries where growth is imminent. Supply side versus Keynesian economics is just the tip of the iceberg in today's global economy.

My biggest issue with most of our leaders is their constant focus on archaic matters of the past. In the 1980s it was the "Cold War". Now it's the "War on Terror". The "War on Terror" is as much a war as the "War on Drugs" was during Reagan's presidency. Neither of them are conflicts of definitive victory. What I mean is that winning the war on terror doesn't exist because you will always have evil people who want to do harm to the innocent. We fight crime in the United States with trained law enforcement, but we haven't declared a war on crime! In fact, we still have crimes; don't we? We still have robberies, murders, and kidnappings; don't we? There is no such thing as winning the war on crime. You fight to minimize it! Same holds true for the war on drugs. We fight to minimize the impact of drugs on our communities. Terrorism is the same way. We must fight to minimize its impact on the global community. That's why you engage your allies and don't act unilaterally in your foreign policy objectives. You don't spend exorbitant resources on trying to win a war against an idea! That's not sound economics no matter what party you're affiliated with!

What this all boils down to is a return to the fundamentals. It is clear that agriculture is in need of revamping. It is clear that manufacturing is in need of re-tooling. We have to address our energy crisis; and believe me, it is a crisis! Instead of investing trillions of dollars in overseas wars, can you imagine where we would be if we began investing those dollars in 2003 on the new green economy? Where would job growth be today?

Every day that we spend bickering over useless political buzzwords, we give up ground to the Chinese. Every day we spend borrowing money to help prop up an economy that hasn't invested in its greatest asset (the people) is a dollar wasted. We can find ways to restore balance to our economy and progress to a more promising future, or we can continue down the path of petty bickering and archaic national policy toward economic irrelevance. America…I'm talking to you!

Chapter 6
Whose Country is this?

"All authority belongs to the people"
Thomas Jefferson, 3rd President of the United States

Thomas Jefferson fought fiercely for this throughout his political career. He was a proponent of republicanism (not to be confused with the Republican Party), stressing liberty and inalienable rights. This country should always answer to the people and not the few. Often, I think that many of the politicians of today forget this fact. There is a lack of courage on the part of some to do the right thing as it pertains to the direction of the country and most importantly the vitality of the middle class. Lobbyists with incredible wealth continue to dominate the political debate. Issues that were so important in the recent presidential election of 2008 continue to be buried by the selfish greed of the elite corporations. No better example can be found than with the debate over taxes.

There are those who will say that tax cuts create a stimulus for the economy. The idea is that if you lower the effective tax rate of every individual, they will go out and spend the money thus providing a natural stimulus to the economy. While in the short term that may be true, the biggest issue with that line of thinking is that traditionally spending is not done by the top 5% of the country. Individuals in those upper income brackets typically pocket their tax savings. Moreover, many in the top 5% do not even pay the marginal income tax rate that they would traditionally fall into since most make their money on interest and capital gains. In the meantime, the federal government has forgone much needed revenue to close their budget deficit and have not gotten the money back in the form of consumer spending. With unemployment hovering around 9%, you are also losing out on additional tax revenue because one tenth of your population is not paying taxes on their wages. The money in the form of tax cuts has effectively gone into a vacuum, much like the money we have spent on the two wars in the Middle East.

 Consumer spending is usually done by the middle class because those are the individuals who have to work to put kids through college, or get their son or daughter braces, or make renovations to their homes to increase their value. You would think that policies to improve the country would be centered on those individuals, but unfortunately this country does not belong to you. It belongs to the rich, and thus democracy has been replaced by *corporatocracy*. None of what I see has anything to do with sound economic policy. What this amounts to is a corrupt political culture where our leaders do nothing to revive the economy for the people that matter and instead choose to shy away from the responsibility of protecting the jobs of our citizens. It cost too much to spend money on improving roads, bridges, and schools but we spare no expense to preserve the tax cuts of the rich! It costs too much money to protect the jobs of school teachers, firefighters, and union workers but tax cuts for the wealthy…can't let those expire! It reeks of hypocrisy!

If we want to be serious about correcting the issues in this country, we must have an honest discussion about how we got here. I am not talking about the political talking points that you hear on CNN, Fox, or MSNBC. I'm talking about the real reasons behind our economic stagnation and lack of job growth. When you hear political banter between both sides of the political aisles, you hear arguments about Fannie Mae and Freddie Mac. You hear extensive debate about tax policy. You almost certainly hear a discussion about the deficit or spending record of either political party. Nobody talks about the structural issues that exist within our economy.

The purchasing power of the middle class has been obliterated by the corporate terrorism that exists in today's America. Wages have not kept up with the growth in the economy that began in the 90's. This issue was never addressed when former President George W Bush was in office, and currently President Barack Obama would like to begin the process of tackling this issue and has been stonewalled by Republican opposition. Corporations have been able to save money over the last ten to fifteen years with the advent of new technology and outsourcing. Meanwhile, corporations pocketed the extra savings and never invested in their workforce. Hourly wages flattened in spite of former President Clinton's attempt to raise the minimum wage. Do you know that if you compared the median salary for the typical American male now to the median salary 30 years ago that the American male of today actually makes less? This of course has factored in adjustments for inflation. The quality of life for the average American male today is less than it was 30 years ago. That is sad and pathetic!

I'm sure you're probably asking yourself; didn't we experience great economic growth and prosperity in the 1990's? The answer to that question is yes. That is deceiving though. Though jobs were created in the 1990's you have to remember that the majority of that job growth was women flooding the work force. In the mid-80's, forty one percent of women were working. By the late 1990's that number shot up to sixty percent. This was a coping mechanism for middle class families. Cost of living and real prices had gone up and thus they had to keep up. The necessary result was that the wives decided to help put bread on the table.

The other issue, I should point out at this juncture is the quality of life for the American worker. None of us is working in a literal sweatshop, but we're definitely putting in more hours to make up for the lack of wage increases. The average male is putting in 100 more hours per year and the average female is putting in 200 more hours per year. That directly impacts the structure of the home. Not only that, but it puts undue strain on marital relationships. If you want to know the number one enemy of the institution of marriage in this country, you should look no further than the declining quality of life and lack of wages. The majority of the wealth that was created over the last 10 to 15 years has gone to the top 1% of Americans. According to Robert B Reich, former United States Secretary of Labor under President Clinton, the top 1% of Americans took 23.5% of the nation's total income in 2007. That same group only took in 9% of the nation's total income in the late 1970's.

Why even bring any of this up? What is the point of me rehashing these statistics? The broader question I'm trying to answer here is "whose country is this?" It has become increasingly apparent that this country doesn't belong to the people. It belongs to the corporations. They are the ones who employ people (or enslave people depending on how you view it), create the products that we all use, and influence the political landscape. The Supreme Court has even guaranteed that corporations would have unsurpassed power to influence the political landscape with one ruling. Now corporations can contribute as much money as they would like to political candidates during elections. This unprecedented ruling has given corporations the ability to hold the political process hostage for their own selfish interests. I am not against corporations having a seat at the table to voice their interests. I am against corporations having such undue influence that it crowds out the interests of the rest of society. As it stands now, there is no way for the common man to compete with the shouts and screams of corporate dollars.

      The founding fathers spoke at great length about the federal government not overstepping their boundaries. They stated that if left unchecked the federal government would grow into a monstrosity that usurps the individual rights and liberties of man. Often you'll hear Libertarians and Tea Party candidates refer back to this point. I for one agree that the federal government has certain responsibilities to the general welfare of its citizens; however, the federal government must limit the scope of its power so as to prevent the degradation of individual rights and liberties. Fortunately, we have a system of checks and balances between the three branches of government to prevent this monstrosity from taking shape. Moreover we have a two party system of government which allows the potential for useful debate to take place between varied points of view. My question is what would the founding fathers say about the unchecked power of multinational corporations in today's political landscape? I think we can agree that anything that usurps the power of the people should be challenged. We want to defend the tactics of corporations under the guise of free enterprise, but there is nothing free about what they have been able to impose upon the American citizens for the last twenty to thirty years.

    I mentioned that our democracy has been replaced with a *corporatocracy*. Democracy comes from the Greek word dēmokratía (*rule of the people*). When corporate interests take the power away from the people, you can no longer call it a democracy. Power now rests with entities that aren't even limited to this country anymore. Multinational corporations operate in dozens if not hundreds of countries around the world. Their network of power to influence government policy is not confined to the United States. John Perkins wrote a book called "Confessions of an Economic Hitman" in 2004. In it he wrote about his responsibility to influence outcomes that were favorable to large multinational corporations and the United States government. What that tells me is that greed is at the heart of every move that corporations make. There is no difference with their grip on Washington. The interests of the general public are meaningless and the selfish intent of the corporations has become paramount to the general welfare of the American citizen.

I have told some of my friends that there is no courage in leadership today. I hate to paint it with a broad brush like that because I know that there are some individuals who are trying to make a difference, but forgive me if I'm a little jaded. Nobody does anything today because it is the right thing to do. Everything is about political gamesmanship and posturing. Concrete debate doesn't happen anymore to solve complex issues. Leaders don't answer to the people who elected them. Instead they answer to the dollars that paid for their campaign. This points to another issue of campaign finance reform; an issue that could be discussed in a book all by itself.

America...I'm Talking to You

Tom Browkaw dubbed the generation that lived through the great depression as the greatest generation. He supported his argument with an assessment that described their willingness to do the right thing; not because they wanted fame or recognition, but because it was the right thing to do. He talked about how they came back from World War 2 and rebuilt this country into a superpower again. There are those who are in the baby boomer generation who also mention that their contributions to civil rights should not be overlooked. One could also argue that it was their contribution to segregation which precipitated the events of civil rights in the first place, but that is neither here nor there. What is the legacy of the baby boomer generation? It's a great question. I think the jury is still out on the transformative impact that baby boomers have had on this country.

The reason I can say that the jury is still out on this question is because baby boomers are still influencing the policies of today. I respect everything they have done, however I think it is time to allow the next greatest generation to shape the future of this country. What's clear is that the current model is no longer sustainable in the 21st century. The oldest members of the generation known simply as "Gen Y" or the "Millenials" are now 10 – 12 years into their professional careers. Due to the technological age they have lived through, they have been able to access more information in their formative years than most baby boomers have in the 60 plus years they have been governing this nation. I am sure that there may be some of you who are reading this and saying that you vehemently disagree with me on this point, but I think that due to the positive social changes that were shaped by the baby boomer generation, they may feel it is their right to collect.

Before you label me an anti-baby boomer leftist liberal, let me explain what I mean by that comment. Over the last 10 – 15 years, we have seen spending on education, infrastructure, and environmental improvement diminish proportionally to increases in spending on healthcare and public pensions. Those two areas are directly going to impact the baby boomers over the next 10 to 15 years as many of them begin to retire. What is going on is that we are betting the future of our country against the short term comfort of baby boomers. This is happening everywhere; not just here in the United States. Amidst financial insolvency in Greece, there were protests when the government began to propose an increase in the retirement age thus giving them an additional 2 years to pay out pensions to retired workers. The retirement age is currently 61. The Greek government was proposing raising it to 63. Germany's chancellor had a similar proposal in the works until the manufacturing sector began to flourish. In both cases the baby boomers threatened with their protests and ability to influence the outcome of elections and thus those proposals were quickly defeated.

    What is interesting is that the current debate about fiscal responsibility and taxes is all smoke and mirrors. The underlying concern is that members of congress don't want to make important and much needed investment in the future. That's why you see budget cuts in every state as it pertains to teachers and education funding. That's why environmental initiatives like cap and trade are being demonized. The green economy that President Obama mentioned in his campaign is being characterized as a phantom industry that will not create a single job. That is why a bill will be proposed to fix highways and infrastructure around the country and they will delay and cry about the budget deficit while advocating tax cuts for the richest Americans. They don't want any funding going to things that will invest in the future of this country and thus the future of the children they claim that they are fighting for.

I ask again, whose country is this? The election of 2008 was a transformational moment. As I said before, it was a paradigm shift in the geopolitical thought in this country. There was a strong presence from the millenials, but it seems like there is a quiet discontent from them on issues that are happening in Washington. I wrote a song in 2008, called "Hey Young World" and essentially it was a call to the youth of America to get involved in their civic duty. It called for them to collectively wake up from the slumber of apathy and do something to make a difference in the lives of others. I wrote a reprise in 2010 called "Young World Gotta Wake Up" because I wanted to remind them again about what is at stake. We have seen the spirit of the Gen Y in the aftermath of the earthquake in Haiti. Numerous social media websites were galvanized around the purpose of raising money for the cause. You saw how everyone got involved in sending a text message to raise money for the victims. Locally, I saw many of my friends that I went to high school and college with who organized concerts and social gatherings to raise money and garner support.

    I can appreciate where the discontent is coming from. There is a general feeling that we don't have a seat at the table when it comes to influencing policy in this country. There are things that are important to us and our future in this great nation that are being ignored. This country really needs a facelift and we're ready to do the necessary plastic surgery, but we feel as though there are those who want to keep us out of the operating room. In the midst of all this talk about establishment candidates being rooted out of Washington, I'm not seeing an actual change in policies as much as I'm seeing a shift to the right or left of the political spectrum. It is still the recycled ideas of the past. Everything is being approached as Keynesian versus Supply Side; Pro-choice versus Pro-life; Big government versus little government. I'm sitting back and I'm saying to myself, these guys are approaching policy analysis like two people having a debate about what to wear in the fall. What I mean by that is we are in the fall season and instead of trying to figure what is the appropriate thing to wear, you have two people arguing between shorts and a tank-top or a winter coat with gloves! The real answer is neither of you is right. That is what I'm saying to people on either extreme of the political sphere. The issues of today are not summer versus winter ideas. The issues of today are more like the fall or spring where it is not clear what we need to be doing, so it's imperative that we have useful dialogue about the issues.

We can ill-afford to sit back and wait for the existing leadership to figure it out for themselves. Young world we have to wake up and mobilize to the front line. As David Smith, founder and executive director of mobilize.org said, democracy is an unfinished project in need of an upgrade. As citizens we are called to be the leaders of today. We need to reform the way we do things and the only way to do that is to be vigilant in our intent and focused on the results that we desire. Mahatma Gandhi once said that we must become the change that we want to see in the world. It is imperative that we take his advice to heart and begin to mold the country back into the image of the founding fathers. It's time for us to take back the country from the grip of the corporate elite. We need to reinvigorate our democracy and drive a stake into the heart of *corporatocracy*! America…I'm Talking to you!

Chapter 7
The Future Starts Today

"Don't stop thinking about tomorrow! Don't stop, it'll soon be here! It'll be better than before! Yesterday's gone, Yesterday's gone!" ~Fleetwood Mac

This song was written by vocalist and keyboard player Christine McVie. She admits that she wrote it in the aftermath of her divorce with then husband John McVie. It was meant to be an optimistic view on a difficult end to an eight year marriage. The song most notably was used by former President Bill Clinton in his 1992 campaign. He was trying to capture the same hope and optimism against the backdrop of a recession the country was in. I'd like to point out the most important line in that song to me. You find it at the end of the song where it says "don't look back". I don't think it means never look back because at times it is necessary to look back and learn from mistakes. The key is whether or not you dwell on the past. If we are going to move successfully into the 21st Century, we are going to have to let go of the past way of doing things. Yesterday's gone! Yesterday's gone!

The first thing we are going to have to do is change the social construct. Most of us were not born into money and therefore, the only way to level the playing field is to give access to education. Not only should early childhood education be a strong emphasis, but education at all levels needs to be a strong emphasis. I tried to look for tuition free universities in the United States and after an extensive search I found one. Berea College in Berea Kentucky is the only college in the entire country that is tuition free. They primarily admit students from the Appalachian region, but they also have admitted students from abroad. Their student body represents 60 countries and all 50 states in the US. I found it interesting that although this school was founded in the south, the founder John G. Fee was adamant about having a school that was anti-slavery and pro-Christian values. It makes sense because when you say you have Christian values, you shouldn't then be in favor of enslaving your fellow man, but I digress from my point. This school has been in existence for over 150 years and my question is this...how is it that they have survived all of these years without charging their students a single dime?

The answer is quite simple actually. Since students are able to go to the school tuition free, when they graduate they become very disciplined donors to the school. Not only that, but the parents are disciplined donors to the university as well. Because they have used their endowment responsibly, they have been able to sustain this long standing tradition. To them, it's not about greed. It's about providing the best liberal arts education to its students so that they become productive members of society. Of course there are student fees and room and board, but if you look at the totality of college education, those expenses are minimal in comparison to the tuition costs. I'm wondering why Berea College is the only college in the entire United States that has this structure. It is apparent that the only way to close the gap in the social construct is to give appropriate access to higher education. Studies have proven that this is an indicator of a higher quality of life.

Unfortunately, everything in this country is about making money. There is very little emphasis on the public good. Corporations want to make money so everything they do is centered on that goal. Schools want to have these huge endowments and entitlements to their sports programs, deans, and chancellors so they charge exorbitant tuition fees...more money! In our states, the local government requires that we pay property taxes on our houses and heaven forbid that they lower the property taxes when your house loses value...more money! It's funny that in college, economics and public policy management courses talk about total utility and public good, but we never quite get the concept to play out in real life. Meanwhile, we get into debt to get this education and spend the rest of our lives paying it off. We can never quite get around to earning and saving the income so that we can close the wealth gap in this country. It's no wonder that poverty levels are the highest they've been in over 15 years.

We also have to refocus on improving median incomes in this country. It is ridiculous to think that by giving huge tax cuts to the super rich that the wealth is going to trickle down to the rest of us. If that really worked, then between 2001 and now we would have seen median incomes go up but that has not happened. If tax cuts for the super wealthy were really an economic stimulus, then we would have seen incredible job growth from 2001 until now and we would have seen more consistent and sustained growth in GDP. Of course, we can say definitively that wealth has not trickled down despite the Bush-era tax cuts that have been in place since 2001. Those who advocate such policies need to realize that yesterday's gone and those policies didn't work, and they won't work in the future. We must not continue to do the same things over and over, hoping that the outcomes will be different – the truly classical definition of insanity. Let's get off the path of insanity and move on to the sanity of prosperity.

The next step toward the future of this nation is improving the cultural relationships that we have in this country. In November 2008 we elected the first African American President of the United States. It was truly an historic occasion that made me very proud. The reason for my pride stemmed from the fact that this country put aside any differences that they had and rallied around a man whose story was much like any one of us. For the first time, it seemed that the content of someone's character was being judged and not the color of their skin. This slowly deteriorated shortly after the inauguration as political battle lines were drawn in the sand. Doubts about the President's ability to lead became common place. There was growing determination to ensure that anything that he wanted to accomplish would not get done. The voices of people challenging the legitimacy of Barack Obama's presidency began to grow louder and garner more attention as accusations were stated about his place of birth. A growing number of individuals were beginning to believe that the President was not Christian and in fact was Muslim (as if there should be something wrong with the faith someone professes anyway). To make a long story short, any good vibes I had from the election and inauguration was soon wiped out.

    Personally, I have been fortunate enough to be exposed to many cultures. In addition, I have a strong curiosity about other cultures and religions. This curiosity causes me to read more about other cultures and religions because I find that I can relate to things better when I understand them. Many of the cultural rifts that we see in this country stem from a lack of understanding of one another. If you go back to the civil rights era and Jim Crow, you'll find that a lot of the hidden prejudice people had came from myths that were perpetrated by people who were deemed to be experts in science, psychology, and sociology. There were scientists who were publishing studies that made claims about the inferiority of blacks in terms of their intellect and even life expectancy. These findings were shared over and over again. Of course, if you tell a lie over and over again with any measure of consistency, it becomes your truth.

If people really took the time to realize that we are more alike than we are different, we probably wouldn't have so many issues. In the first place, we have been able to trace the origins of man to Africa. There are some people who don't want to admit this or deal with this reality. They'd rather act as if this is an untrue statement. Dr. Albert Chuchward, a distinguished scholar, archaeologist, and anthropologist has theorized that the earliest human species appeared nearly 2 million years ago in the great lakes region of central Africa. This species would inhabit the entire African continent. Further discussion on the subject involved a 1988 article "The Search for Adam & Eve" traced a trail of DNA which led to the conclusion that we could all be traced back to a single woman. That woman, Eve, is believed to have lived in Sub-Saharan Africa some 80,000 to 200,000 years ago. These descendants began to inhabit the entire world. So even for Christians, looking to identify where they came from, our lineage traces back to Africa. This is widely accepted as genetic fact.

If you're European, your ancestry began in Africa. If you're Asian, your ancestry began in Africa. If you're American Indian, South American, or Aborigine, your ancestry began in Africa. Why do we have such a difficult time relating to each other? The answer is simple. What we don't understand, we vilify. We see it now in so many different dynamics that it is almost commonplace. Nasir Jones, also known as Nas, stated it best in his lyric..."people fear what they can't understand, hate what they can't conquer; guess it's just a theory of man!" I suppose our defense mechanism when we're dealing with the religion of Islam is to vilify it when we don't understand it. Perhaps it is a defense mechanism to hate it because it is so different and our knowledge of it is so limited, but this is not the right coping mechanism. Stephen Covey was the one who said "seek first to understand, and then seek to be understood". If we do this more consistently then we can have more useful dialogue with one another and eventually come together more appropriately to build this nation.

One thing that would make a world of difference in this country would be for us to end the hypocrisy that we see in our politics. I wonder about the individuals who talk about spending billions of dollars on stimulating the economy, but fall silent when we're spending billions of dollars on unwarranted wars overseas. I'm curious when people talk about the size of government and it's intrusion into our lives when we pass health insurance reform, but are OK with having a law pass that would allow the government to prohibit a woman's ability to get an abortion. Where were the constitutionalists of the Tea Party when our fourth amendment rights were being violated in the misuse of the FISA bill? These are all valid questions. I'm sure that the individuals who I'm questioning have legitimate reasons for why they believe what they believe. It doesn't change the fact that I feel that it is hypocritical.

Some of these things are head scratchers. I suppose I just don't get it. Maybe if the media weren't so tacitly involved in the deception we wouldn't have this issue. We boast about having an independent media in this country, but so much of that has been affected in the last 10 years. Every news program now is an op-ed. We don't report facts anymore. We merely report opinions and sound bytes. It's amazing that people aren't more intuitive about things. Maybe I'm that way because my parents have always been that way. Nothing at the surface level is acceptable to me unless I've had a chance to research it and think about it. Today, our society blindly follows what is said on television as if it is gospel truth. We need to have a level of skepticism about what we see on television. Let's face it, if the government answers to corporations, who do you think the media answers to? We have seen an incredible consolidation of media conglomerates over the last 20 years. All of these conglomerates need to make profit and this profit is generated through ad revenue. If you don't think this influences their ability to be unbiased then you're being naïve.

Sources these days aren't checked and typically they are biased. It used to be that you had to verify your sources before an editor or news producer would accept putting your story in print or on the air. In today's fast paced 24-hour news cycle, reporters resort to using social media for sources. You'll find that some reporters use online blogs and twitter feeds as a source and will go on the air with this without double checking the facts! Perhaps this is a result of the incredible influence that the corporate elite have on the dissemination of news. Rupert Murdoch the CEO of News Corp admitted that when he had a meeting with President Barack Obama, the President complained about how he was being portrayed on Fox News. Murdoch admitted that he was doing that in retaliation because the President did not readily have a meeting with Murdoch shortly after winning the election. This obviously has nothing to do with facts but had everything to do with his ego. I'm not sure how that is justifiable, but at the end of the day you are influencing the thoughts and opinions of the people who watch your programming. It's irresponsible at best! When you hear a story like that, how can you believe in the independence of the media? How can you even believe that what you are being told is factual? These are things that we need to correct as a nation. As a country that is focused on democracy and freedom, our press should be free from bias and corporate interests.

I talked earlier about the egalitarian philosophy that our founding fathers used as the basis for our constitution. The consistent reference to the fact that we have inalienable rights endowed by our creator is the backdrop for the moral principles of this country. There are those who are critics of the egalitarian philosophy because they feel it undercuts the individuality and talent of people. They argue that if we focus on egalitarian principles at their core, we somehow penalize those who are talented, innovative, or intelligent enough to excel in certain areas. I think these individuals have confused the intent. The egalitarian philosophy doesn't try to equalize the amount of what people have; instead it tries to equalize the opportunity that each person is given to attain and achieve. It was the same philosophy that was applied in the case of school integration in the mid to late 1950's. When the Supreme Court ruled in the case of Brown v. Board of Education, they determined that segregated schools were unconstitutional. The court ruled unanimously against segregated schools because in their view separate educational facilities were inherently unequal. The court wasn't ruling on talent or resources themselves, but they were ruling on the opportunity to attend the same facilities. There's a difference. Egalitarian viewpoints preserve the very essence of what makes this country great.

I'd like to see our political leadership return to this way of governing. I've felt this way for quite some time now. To be honest, I see that we still have a long way to go before that is possible. There are so many entrenched ideological divides that it is often very difficult to get people to agree on anything. It amazes me when I speak to some individuals how unwilling they are to listen to another's point of view. It's as if, whatever they believe is right and they don't care whether what you're saying even makes sense. The corporations influence the politicians to perpetuate those rifts, and the media feeds into it by adding fuel to the proverbial fire.

The seal of the United States counters this sentiment of divisiveness and rancor. On it the words *e pluribus unum* - out of many one, are inscribed. The literal translation is even more powerful than the one most of us have come to know and understand. In the Latin, e pluribus unum describes an action, so that when translated it actually means, many uniting into one! It is apparent that we are required to act out of selflessness toward one another. Egalitarian principles are thus not a socialist call to government takeover, but a call to take care of our brother or sister. It is a call to love our neighbor as ourselves. When many people unite into one, mountains can be moved; lives can be changed; enemies can be toppled. When many people unite into one, we can defeat the evil Third Reich of Germany to prevent the ethnic cleansing of millions of Jews, Gypsies, and Jehovah's Witnesses. When many people unite into one, we can defeat the stain of Jim Crow and emerge as a country that can elect its first African American president. When many people unite into one, we can solve some of the most complex issues of the 21st century.

Wouldn't it be nice if we could focus on the fact that what divides us is minute in the grand scheme of things? Wouldn't it be nice if we could focus on the Latin phrase e. pluribus unum? Simply put...out of many one...America...I'm Talking to you!

Chapter 8
Closing Remarks

"I'm saying, let's focus on rebuilding. Stop with all the bickering; we have got to teach our children. Create more jobs for the struggling poor; help the middle class so that they can truly afford! ~excerpt from Closing Remarks on my 2008 album America...I'm Talking to You

I wanted to close by sharing a few anecdotes about a few topics of interest. I didn't necessarily want to devote entire chapters to them because in a sense they all work together as a summation of this book. Hopefully, you'll respect my decision to discuss them here. There are three main topics that I'd like to highlight in my closing remarks...religion, people and politics. After discussing these topics, I'll offer my final comment.

In bringing up religion, people and politics, I chuckle to myself because we have a tendency to loosely associate religion with the republican party and an agnostic or atheist viewpoint with the democratic party. It's almost as if, someone like me doesn't exist. I am someone who has conservative values in some respects; however when it comes to social responsibility and the public good I am more liberal. The point being that my party affiliation should not cause someone to make quick assumptions about what I think and feel. I am a complex person as many individuals are. How I feel can vary based on the day you happen to catch me or events that may have happened to me over the course of my life. You'll find that many rags to riches millionaires still identify with the plight of the people that they once knew. Though Sean Carter (a.k.a. Jay-Z) might be on pace to be a billionaire in 2014, he will tell you that he still votes in the interest of those in the Marcy projects of Brooklyn, New York. Experiences often shape us but they don't necessarily define us.

Religion also shapes our individual thoughts and moral standings. Whether you are Christian, Jewish, Muslim, Buddhist, or Hindu, you have developed a set of core values based on what your religious tenets have taught you. The founding fathers of this country clearly believed in God. The language that they used…inalienable rights endowed by our creator; all men were created equal; each of these phrases speaks to a fundamental belief in a God who created us in his image. Their belief in such a creator shaped how they wanted us to relate to each other, but they did not want it to shape how we structured our government, policies, or laws.

Religion itself has a long and storied history as it pertains to government. There is so much debate about the separation of church and state today. The debate spans from prayer in schools to a statue of the 10 commandments outside of a state building in Alabama. I think John F. Kennedy addressed it best when he spoke in front of the Greater Houston Ministerial Association on September 12, 1960. He spoke of an America where the leaders did not answer to the pope or to protestant ministers of the faith. The question is what did the founding fathers mean by separation of church and state? If I were to put it in one phrase, I would say this. The founding fathers did not want government to sponsor one religion over another. They had seen what happens when that is the case. The crusades in Europe were a Christian crusade to reclaim the holy land and dominate Islamic nations. This is what happens when government is too heavily invested in the religion of their nation. It causes them to make policy decisions that are detrimental to the nation overall.

This doesn't mean that public displays of religion are prohibited or wrong. In fact we are encouraged by our constitutional rights to practice our religion freely. As people we need to cherish our religious freedom, while preserving that wall of separation that Thomas Jefferson spoke of. It surprises me how much emphasis we put on a presidential candidate's faith, when we are trying to create that separation. Their faith becomes more important than their stance on the issues and this can present many problems. The complexities of religion and politics are not black and white.

I find it terribly disconcerting when people look at every issue as black and white. In this life there is so much gray in so many issues that it is unbelievable. The issues that should be black and white; however are the ones that we make exceptions for. An example of a black and white issue is crime. If you commit a crime, then you have to accept the appropriate level of punishment for the crime. That doesn't always happen. We find that if you are a celebrity or a well connected entrepreneur there is a much different legal system for you than the guy who lives in the projects of Detroit,

Michigan. We try to make excuses for these individuals when they do something wrong. The excuse is that they have psychological issues or they had a rough upbringing. I am not discounting that those things can affect us, but let's face it, I listened to gangster hip-hop when I was growing up, but I never once thought it would be a good idea to get a gun and shoot someone. At some point we can't say that it's someone else's fault that I ended up the way I did. We need to take responsibility for our own actions and accept the consequences of those actions.

Do you want to know what is not a black and white issue? Education reform is not a black and white issue. Fixing the economy is no longer a black and white issue; in fact, I'm not sure it ever was a black and white issue. The problem I see is that we treat issues like religion and politics, education and the economy as if they are black and white issues in the media. We treat them as if they are black and white issues in political campaigns when in reality they have very real and complex implications in the lives of everyday citizens.

Our politics in this nation must change. Barack Obama gave a keynote speech at the 2004

Democratic National Convention. He spoke of America in these terms.

> "there's not a liberal America and a conservative America - there's the United States of America. There's not a black America and white America and Latino America and Asian America; there's the United States of America. The pundits like to slice-and-dice our country into Red States and Blue States; Red States for Republicans, Blue States for Democrats. But I've got news for them, too. We worship an awesome God in the Blue States, and we don't like federal agents poking around our libraries in the Red States. We coach Little League in the Blue States and have gay friends in the Red States. There are patriots who opposed the war in Iraq and patriots who supported it. We are one people, all of us pledging allegiance to the stars and stripes, all of us defending the United States of America."

This is the America I'm calling on us to be. The type of America that will look at the issues of the 21st century and say that we can look into the next frontier and create an America that is better for future generations of Americans. We need to have an America that has a renewed sense of purpose to help the middle class get back on its feet. We need an America that says we will not accept the status quo any longer. We need an America that doesn't resort to petty bickering and works together on one accord to find meaningful solutions. In this new America, we will allow the next great generation of Americans to have a voice in shaping our country's future. In this new America, we won't look at people who don't look like us as enemies of the state, but as brothers and sisters who matter. Finally this America will look like the last best hope for prosperity and freedom; a beacon of light for nations around the world to look up to!

America…I'm done talking to you…for now!

Epilogue

When I wrote the songs for the album America...I'm Talking to You in 2008, my inspiration for that album was the potential candidacy of then Senator Barack Obama. I was inspired by the possibilities. I wondered what it would do for so many African American young men in this country. As the events unfolded, I was happy to see that not only did he receive the Democratic nomination, but I was hopeful that if elected, he would usher in a new era of politics. I was hoping for the type of politics that would push aside the urge for partisan rancor. I was looking to see if he would be able to follow through on many of the principles that he espoused in his critically acclaimed book The AUDACITY of HOPE.

Who could have envisioned all that would unfold in the years following his inauguration? Who could have seen the type of vitriol that would cause such gridlock in our political system? Seeing such difficult circumstances where it seems almost impossible to move this country forward has brought us to the brink of social chaos. Protests are going on from both sides of the aisles. The Tea Party is calling for a Constitutional Convention and I'm pretty sure the Occupy Wall Street group is not too far behind with similar calls. In the midst of all this, I was asked to run for local office and there are some who wonder if I've lost my mind. Why on earth would I want to run for political office in such dire circumstances; at a time when the public's confidence in government as a whole is at an all time low? Why would I want to run for the board of chosen Freeholders in Somerset County, NJ; a county which has not elected a democrat to the board of chosen Freeholders in 32 years. The answer is simple…I believe that elections should be about the skill, background, and vision of the candidate. The party affiliation is merely the general platform of that individual. In order to really understand how that individual will govern, you have to get to know them. That's what is missing in all of our dialogue as of late.

    I sincerely hope and believe that it will change for the better. I sincerely hope and believe that with everything that is going on right now, the people will right the ship of this country and set us on a course for prosperity and growth in the future. My only task is to continue to push for the ideals that will make this country better. No matter what, I'll keep pushing.

Notes

OPENING REMARKS

Song lyrics taken from *Opening Remarks* off of the album America...I'm Talking to You. © WJV Music Group, LLC. BMI Music Publishing

WHO AM I

Excerpt taken from Psalm 139:14 NIV, *I praise you because I am fearfully and wonderfully made; your works are wonderful, I know that full well.*

WE THE PEOPLE

Transcript of the Constitution of the United States of America taken from http://www.archives.gov/exhibits/charters/constitution_transcript.html

Mark Bittman, New York Times, Why We're Fasting, March 29, 2011

Paul Krugman, New York Times, Now That's Rich, August 22, 2010

David Leonhardt, New York Times, Tax Cuts That Make a Difference, August 31, 2010

POLITICS AS USUAL

John Perkins, "Confessions of an Economic Hitman", Berrett-Koehler Publishers (November 9, 2004)

Understanding Social Problems. Cengage Lerning. 2009.p. 256

The new Global Economy by Noam Chomsky (http://www.thirdworldtraveler.com/Chomsky/ChoOdon_GlobEcon.html)

The World Distribution of Household Wealth (http://www.iariw.org/papers/2006/davies.pdf) study by Davies et al.

John Perkins (author) lecture on Corporatocracy (http://www.johnperkins.org/?page_id=9)

Andy Webster, New York Times, Thoughts on a 'Corporatocracy' (http://www.nytimes.com/2008/08/15/movies/15apol.html)

IT WAS ALL A DREAM

Selected Letters from Abraham Lincoln, Letter to William Elkins, http://www.ratical.org/corporations/Lincoln.html

Master Slave Morality, Wikipedia, http://en.wikipedia.org/wiki/Master-slave_morality

Knowledge for Development Program, World Bank

Book: The Knowledge-Based Economy in Central and East European Countries

Bell, D. (1974). The Coming of Post-Industrial Society: A Venture in Social Forecasting. London: Heinemann

Drucker, P. (1993). Post-Capitalist Society. Oxford: Butterworth Heinemann

Chichilnisky, Graciela, The Knowledge Revolution, Columbia University (1998) The Journal of International Trade & Economic Development

Hearn, Greg et al., "Information Society Policy", Knowledge Policy: Challenges for the 21st Century

WHOSE COUNTRY IS THIS

Teaching for Democracy in an Age of Corporatocracy (http://www.eric.ed.gov/ERICWebPortal/search/detailmini.jsp?_nfpb=true&_&ERICExtSearch_SearchValue_0=EJ825486&ERICExtSEarch_SearchType_0=no&accno=EJ825486) by Christine E. Sleeter, Teachers College, Columbia University

Alex: Corporations and Propaganda (http://www.radio4all.net/index.php/program/4041)

The Corporation, 2003 (http://www.thecorporation.com)

Nafeez Mosaddeq Ahmed, Why The Media Lie, The Corporate Structure of the Mass Media

THE FUTURE STARTS TODAY

David Brooks, New York Times, Talent Magnet, January 24, 2011

Martin Fackler, New York Times, In Japan, Young Face Generational Roadblocks, January 27, 2011

CLOSING REMARKS

American Rhetoric: A speech by State Senator Barack Obama at 2004 Democratic National Convention.
http://www.americanrhetoric.com/speeches/convention2004/barackobama2004dnc.htm

Acknowledgments

I'd like to thank my wonderful parents Dr. Agber Ifan and Zanenge Ifan for supporting every endeavor of mine; from music to sports to ministry. I'd like to thank my siblings Justice Ifan and Victoria Ifan for continuing to inspire me each and every day. Hopefully I am the kind of brother that you are proud of. I'd like to thank Nicole Simpson for writing the forward of this book. Of course this couldn't be possible without the talent and ingenuity entrusted to me by Father God. I am thankful to him from whom all blessings flow. It is my sincerest hope that I have made the Lord proud with this work that he has given me to share with the world. Thank you to everyone who has supported this book and will support it in the future. These are just my thoughts ladies and gentlemen; just what I was feeling at the time! I hope it inspires useful debate.

www.ingramcontent.com/pod-product-compliance
Lightning Source LLC
Chambersburg PA
CBHW072209170526
45158CB00002BA/508